Undoing Ties

Undoing Ties

Political Philosophy at the
Waning of the State

Mariano Croce and Andrea Salvatore

Bloomsbury Academic
An imprint of Bloomsbury Publishing Inc

B L O O M S B U R Y
NEW YORK • LONDON • NEW DELHI • SYDNEY

Bloomsbury Academic

An imprint of Bloomsbury Publishing Inc

1385 Broadway	50 Bedford Square
New York	London
NY 10018	WC1B 3DP
USA	UK

www.bloomsbury.com

BLOOMSBURY and the Diana logo are trademarks of Bloomsbury Publishing Plc

Orginally published as "Filosofia politica. Le nuove frontier"
© 2012 Gius. Laterza & Figli
All rights reserved
This English language translation © Mariano Croce and Andrea Salvatore, 2015

Library of Congress Cataloging-in-Publication Data
A catalog record for this book is available from the Library of Congress.

ISBN:	HB:	978-1-6289-2203-5
	PB:	978-1-6289-2202-8
	ePUB:	978-1-6289-2205-9
	ePDF:	978-1-6289-2204-2

Typeset by Fakenham Prepress Solutions, Fakenham, Norfolk NR21 8NN

Contents

Preface to the English Edition

The plurality of forms of life and the threat of instability it poses to political structures has been a constant in human societies. The governance of pluralism and the pursuit of stability have always been major concerns of the theorists of political institutions, from Plato and Aristotle onward. If this holds true, we can hardly say that this book deals with an exceptional and unprecedented transition. Nonetheless, we will claim that, if political philosophy has a reason to exist, this is the capacity to pin down the deep nature of political forms, provide them with justificatory frameworks, explore their distinctive features and foresee their potential developments. It is in this light that we will discuss theoretical paradigms and political theories: we will be looking at their capacity to identify (what we believe to be) one of the key characterizing elements of today's political scenario, that is to say, the reviviscence of sub-state and supra-state groups as crucial political actors vis-à-vis the state. This, according to most of the authors we will examine, will be a strategic political battlefield in the years to come.

The basic aim of this book is to offer an introductory and accessible overview of those paradigms and theories that are specifically concerned with the irreducible plurality of life forms and seek to solve the question of how political institutions could and should accommodate it. As the title of this book signals, it is our claim that a major transition in the field of political philosophy is taking place as the ties between traditional political institutions and citizens are being undone. In this respect, this book is not as much about political transitions as about how political philosophy is reacting to them. This also makes sense of the differences among the chapters of this book. If its structure reflects the particular stance that paradigms and theories take on the way to rethink political institutions (see the Introduction), its leitmotiv is the growing awareness that the pre-eminent role of the main political construction of the last centuries, the state, is undergoing a far-reaching transformation.

It would be pointless to talk about this transformation in the context of this short preface, since the whole book is devoted to it. What we aspire to do here is to highlight that the core of this book is neither the state nor political philosophy, but the relation between them. Modern and contemporary political philosophy have emerged and developed within a political structure – the state – that, whether knowingly or not, they themselves contributed to shaping. If this relation is not conditional and circumstantial, as we believe, what will happen to political philosophy when its constitutive shell is morphing and fading? This book explores this ongoing tension with an eye to bringing out ambiguities and difficulties more than recipes and solutions. We will survey and discuss the proposals that best reflect this tension and, at the same time, are being affected by its effects.

This entails that our journey into some key themes of today's political philosophy will be arbitrary and partial. For if our main focus will be the way in which the erosion of the ties between the state and its citizens is favouring (and is being favoured by) the parallel re-emergence of new mediatory bodies between them, these topics hardly exhaust the spectrum of political issues. Such a selective strategy, however, will be instrumental in isolating and delving into a pressing question that, in our hypothesis, will acquire even greater importance in the next few years. At the same time, however, our concern is not exclusively with the type of pluralism that is known as cultural or religious pluralism. Much as these topics will be thoroughly addressed in this text, the re-emergence of groups in the political life of contemporary society goes farther than that. The increasing political relevance of groups is first and foremost a symptom of a marked historical shift, which is sweeping away the debris of a political horizon – one that postulated an innate connection between the existence of the state as a political form and the peaceful coexistence of social actors. As this shift erodes the idea that the state is the only guarantor of peace and order, politics makes room for other, perhaps still unimaginable, possibilities. However, as we will show as we go along, these possibilities are several: new key political actors can be civic associations, religious and/or ethnic minorities, legal officials, global legal elites, transnational collectives. These are but a few of the political subjects who claim a renewed political role for themselves the moment the state is waning, and contend that the state monopoly on legitimacy should be rethought to accommodate new legislative and administrative bodies.

If our pithy investigation claims to be a handy meta-history of political philosophy *after*, *above* and *without* the state, we cannot achieve this aim within the bounded area of political philosophy. We will assume, as it were, an external point of view, which allows dialectical exchanges with other disciplines. We decided to 'contaminate' our political-philosophical approach with jurisprudential, sociological and anthropological views on the future developments of state legal orders. This contamination is mainly intended to achieve a critical standpoint on those limits of political philosophy which are rooted, as we maintained above, in the tight relation between the latter and the state as its institutional shell. To focus on these limits, the various chapters of the book use different narrative and argumentative styles. Whereas initially the standpoint will chiefly be intra-disciplinary (Chapters 1 and 2), as the focus expands to include inter-disciplinary elements we seek to be more detailed and to zoom in on a limited set of issues (Chapter 3). We believe this to be an important strongpoint of the book: focusing on political-philosophical issues from within the lexica and approaches of other disciplines truly allows a challenge to some rigidities of political philosophy and advances its frontiers.

Many people have helped us in working through our ideas. We want to thank Nunzio Allocca, Renata Badii, Laura Bazzicalupo, Caterina Botti, Marina Calloni, Norbert Campagna, Thomas Casadei, Ignazio Castellucci, Antonio Cerella, Davina Cooper, Luigi Corrias, Lucio Cortella, Dimitri D'Andrea, Piergiorgio Donatelli, Seán Donlan, Alessandro Ferrara, Peter Fitzpatrick, Lyana Francot, Marco Goldoni, Teodoro Klitsche de la Grange, Leonardo Marchettoni, Michael Marder, Reinhard Mehring, Emmanuel Melissaris, Werner Menski, David Nelken, Dennis Patterson, George Pavlakos, Stefano Petrucciani, Andreas Philippopoulos-Mihalopoulos, Walter Privitera, Elena Pulcini, William Scheuerman, Aldo Schiavello, Bas Schotel, Katharina Strecker, Frederik Swennen, William Twining, Marco Ventura, Bald de Vries, Marc de Wilde.

Many thanks to Daniele Archibugi, Geminello Preterossi and Gordon Woodman for believing in the project from the very beginning.

Special thanks to Virginio Marzocchi, whose teachings have been crucial to our intellectual as well as personal biographies.

Our personal gratitude goes to Enrica Braccioni, Vincenzo Rosito, Michele Spanò, Annamaria Vassalle and Valeria Venditti: strange bedfellows.

Introduction

Often in the history of Western thought political philosophy has been called upon to face more or less epochal juridico-political transitions which subverted crystallized theoretical constellations and triggered far-reaching adjustments in the socio-cultural background of Western societies. This book aims to map some of the most recent and most debated political theories which seek to identify and analyse today's transitions.

Despite substantial differences, the theoretical paradigms examined in this book converge on a basic tenet: a radical metamorphosis is impacting on the deep grammar of contemporary politics and is defying the conceptual devices that legal and political scholars had advanced in previous centuries in order to conceptualize the juridico-political framework of state-centred societies. The metamorphosis at stake is affecting a pivotal element of this framework: at present the state – which is to say, the Western system of organization and division of powers that has existed since the end of the Middle Ages – is changing functions, delegating tasks and relinquishing powers. Perhaps, from a historical point of view, it would be more correct to maintain that what at present is being called into question is one of the state's historical configurations, that is, the 'national-territorial state'. This has long represented the basic unit of a 'system of states' emerged, and definitely consolidated, between the Peace of Westphalia (1648) and the two World Wars. In the past three centuries, the state has taken the shape we are familiar with and that has dominated the political imagery of modernity, to the extent that only a few decades ago it was generally considered to be the only conceivable way to organize and structure a political community. The national-territorial state was a wide legislative, judiciary and administrative machinery called upon to ensure the general obser-vance of legal norms (produced and enforced by the state itself) and to supply goods and services (in terms of both personal security and welfare) to a range of individuals (citizens) in return for contributions.

As we will see as we go along, since the end of the twentieth century some of the key features of the national-territorial state have gradually been eroded. States today can no longer be regarded as the exclusive holders of the monopoly on force; nor are they the only source of valid law, let alone the sole guarantors of peace and security. Such far-reaching transformations are affecting every element of the state machinery. The orderly separation of powers that used to regulate the interplay of government, legislature and the adminis-tration of justice is progressively being altered, to such a degree that the boundaries among them tend to shift or even to vanish. As a consequence, conflicts between powers and bureaucratic impasses are not so much exceptions as frequent stumbling blocks to political and legal procedures that deteriorate day by day in most Western jurisdictions.

This book aims to foreground these transitions, which are opening the door to new models of regulation and organization. To achieve that, we will explore various theories which deploy different conceptual frameworks and reach different conclusions. These theories have been classified according to a tripartite scheme: we have grouped together views that believe future societies to be *after* the state (Chapter 1), *above* the state (Chapter 2), or *without* the state (Chapter 3). To turn this division into a set of questions: are theorists called upon to imagine novel forms of organization that, *after the state*, may revive and revise the traditional national-territorial state? Or is it necessary to promote a model of integration *above the state*, which may collaborate with traditional states and supplement their deficiencies? Or should the state be regarded as an expiring entity, which will shortly be replaced by new, unpredicted and perhaps still unpredictable, forms of political organization? These fundamental questions will provide our analysis with a basic guideline, in order for us to examine some of the most debated theoretical paradigms and to fathom their strengths and weaknesses.

It is our contention that the turmoil that is breaking out at the frontiers of present-day political philosophy can be attributed to the considerable degree of ambiguity and instability of current transitions. Nevertheless, in our view, what is leading most theorists to place emphasis on the themes of risk and uncertainty has primarily to do with the end of a project – both theoretical and practical – that in the last century had allowed the national-territorial state to nurture its legitimacy and to keep its hold on society; a project that today should rather be regarded as the texture of a recent past: liberalism as a theory of government and justice is being relocated from the field of political philosophy to the field of the history of culture, the very moment alternative conceptions of government and justice flow through the fissures of its shell (the state) and dissect it from within.

Today liberalism is following in the footsteps of the political frame within which it has developed. Liberalism is morphing into a series of disjointed and composite tools: the transition that leads many theorists to add the prefix 'neo-' to the term 'liberalism' is a symptom that the latter is no longer a political recipe for a fairer society or for a balanced management of political power. Liberalism turns into a set of utensils instrumental in protecting a few individual rights (above all, free enterprise and private property) and discouraging the breach of agreements among private individuals. There is little doubt that such developments (whether they are to blame or to praise) mirror, and at the same time facilitate, the slippery slope towards the end of the state. This is why we have adopted this theme as the leitmotiv of the first chapter. On the one hand we will discuss what today is constitutive of the government, what are its instruments and what are its principal tasks; on the other hand, we will examine what justice is outside the shell of the state, who its guarantor should be and who can utilize its devices.

The slippery slope conducing to the end of the state, however, is not free of obstacles. For one thing, the factor that is considered to be one of the root causes of the metamorphosis described above, globalization, is not as direct a way to a globalized world as observers and commentators used to believe a couple of decades ago. In effect, the path to a new global order is suffering a major setback owing to the financial and military crises that urge domestic governments to intervene. Therefore, the ideal of a global system of organization turns back to the sphere of utopian thinking, leaving behind contradictions and ambiguities. This will be the subject matter of the second chapter: is the financial crisis contributing to the resurrection of the national component of the state, or, on the contrary, is such a revived national component the battering ram for a new and even more invasive strategy to dismantle the state? The analysis of the many faces of globalization will thus lead us to the analysis of theoretical accounts that still keep faith in the creation of a global order (or even a global democracy) able not to eradicate, but to overhaul the state form.

It is undeniable that most of the theoretical paradigms that are debating the issues mentioned thus far make little effort to conceal their Eurocentric (or more generally Western) stigma. This is perhaps one of their most insidious vices that, to some extent, we are inclined to classify as 'transcendental', for this seems to be a condition of possibility for the formulation itself of some political and legal theories. Most often such a Western bias, which unwittingly hides behind them, prevents scholars from acknowledging that their own theoretical framework is founded on a set of intuitions and schemes that are not common patrimony of an alleged humankind. Rather, they are the outcome of a circumscribed geo-historical experience. However, the array of theoretical tools that proved necessary to make sense of a given geo-historical experience cannot be easily disentangled from it. This is the admonishment voiced in the third chapter: if we intend to overcome the innate flaws of the state as a political structure, we are required to pinpoint its geo-historical and socio-cultural coordinates. We should resist the tendency to confuse the history of Western institutions with the history of the world and should employ culture-specific conceptual tools to study and interpret different contexts. On this account, 'without the state' does not want to signify a break with the experience of the state, but the need for a historical and symbolic relocation. Because of this, we decided to place emphasis on a topic that today is compellingly coming to the fore of the international debate, that is, so-called 'legal pluralism'. This is the cradle of many feasible pathways to reform that necessitate an unprejudiced revision of the political forms we are acquainted with, bearing in mind that all changes entail both gains and losses.

To conclude this introduction, we would like to make the claim that the difficulties and ambiguities affecting the range of issues exposed above mark the presence of two major predicaments: the crisis of politics and the crisis of philosophy.

The critical conditions in which politics is caught do not involve the 'neutralization' of the political sphere. It is more accurate to say that the latter is being relocated in other fields, traditionally distinct from politics: as we already noted while addressing the issues of government and justice, one of the main themes of this book is the progressive redistribution of *specifically political competencies* among bodies and agencies that in the past were considered to lie outside the political sphere (however much they were politically relevant). In particular, the law and the market will be depicted as vehicles of new rationalities that remedy the deficiencies of governments, but, at the same time, rob political institutions of their previous competences and tasks. We will illustrate how relevant non-political institutions, such as courts and multinational corporations, come to play a supplementary role (such as the production of binding norms and the making of decisions on key social issues) which often lacks political legitimacy. In this way, politics becomes highly sensitive to technical inputs and severs its ties with the public sphere as a laboratory of political options and courses of action.

Political philosophy seems to follow suit. It no longer serves as a context of wide-ranging reflections on society and gets rid of its task of advancing bold normative claims. Save for a few exceptions, today's political philosophy is most likely to attest to ongoing tendencies and transformations, to produce conceptual instruments with no strong normative claims and to limit itself to describing the dynamics of a changing society.

In truth, the most relevant philosophical-political paradigms of the end of the last century had already gone down that road: authors who were used to grand theories, philosophical idealizations and far-reaching normative claims have recently become far more cautious and have noticeably tempered the ideal scope of their proposals. Perhaps such a downhill slope can be interpreted as an effect of the critique of bygone neo-Enlightenment, charged with being a vehicle for neo-colonial hegemonic prejudices. Be this as it may, this tendency heightens the feeling that contemporary political philosophy, devoid of potent imaginative visions, can no longer claim to be the legitimate heir of modern political philosophy, for the latter was truly able to deploy the theoretical pillars of the modern state and, at the same time, to help it thrive.

In the end, let us outline the interpretive thesis that lies beneath this book. It seems to us that the hallmark of today's political scenario is the widespread reviviscence of groups as key political actors. Most of the philosophical-political theories that we will explore in the subsequent pages throw light on an epochal turn: the dyad state/citizen, typical of the national-territorial framework, is fated to become a historical relic. Today groups are re-emerging as political entities and indispensable mediatory bodies: every individual, before she is a citizen of the state, belongs to something. This book aims to unearth this 'something'. To put it otherwise: what are the groups that are acquiring political relevance? Are they political collectives based on ethnical bonds? Are they communities bound by religious ties? Are they ensembles of actors engaged in the battles of the global civil society? Are they masses of customers operating within the global market? As we will show, if most of the authors examined in the next chapters agree that groups as active political agents are compellingly returning to the fore, the way to conceive and portray them significantly affects the nature, scope and contents of their respective theories.

After the State

Is it up to the state to ensure conditions of justice and equality? In the present chapter we will try to show how this question – which is actually the real cornerstone of the various political theories that marked the second half of the twentieth century – is losing its centrality because of a radical reconfiguration of the relationship between government and justice. Section 1.1 will highlight how government tends more and more to limit itself to providing only minimal standards of regulation and legality, while delegating some key tasks concerning the management of power and the administration of justice to other, mainly non-public, actors. Indeed, on the one hand, it provides ethnic and cultural groups with the basic prerogative of self-government; on the other hand, it entrusts to various institutions (for example, high courts and international courts) the task of coping with the different social demands and claims of justice by taking binding decisions. Section 1.2 will emphasize how this reshaping of public action has led in recent years to completely new and rather ambiguous forms of social justice.

1.1 Theories of government

1.1.1 New forms of liberalism

Liberalism is a political theory founded on the limitation of state power with the aim of safeguarding and guaranteeing the fundamental rights of individuals. As such, it became a distinct political

theory only with the rise of nation states and within their constitutional architecture. State and liberalism, therefore, are strictly
intertwined: the succession of the historical forms of the former is
matched by the evolution of the theoretical versions of the latter,
which is forced to rethink its legacy in order to meet the new
demands arising from the context that it is called upon to regulate
(Fioravanti 2009; Mann 2012).

The tormented history of the last century ends with the triumph
of liberalism as the only modern political theory that goes beyond
the Western world and that has spread globally. Contemporary liberalism, however, has changed radically to adapt to the evolution of the
state in the late twentieth century. The model of an equal inclusion
of *each as an individual* has been replaced by the model of a differentiated recognition of *each as a member of social, ethnic and religious
groups* of very different (and, more often than not, incompatible)
kinds. This shift is mainly due to global trends and political processes
that hugely contribute to reduce the state – that was until then the
undisputed and sovereign policymaker from both a normative and
a descriptive perspective – to the subordinate function of restraining
the centrifugal forces latent in a multicultural society. As a result,
the political success of such a strategy depends ultimately on factual
contingencies.

In what follows, we will seek to account for such a paradigm shift,
by reading it in the light of the key question that lies at the heart
of political liberalism: How can different and equally legitimate
individual interests and demands stand side by side in peaceful
coexistence? According to the traditional answer, what is needed is
a well-defined set of neutral constitutional rules, which are deemed
to be able to ensure a given set of basic rights, enforced to protect
individuals both from others and from the state itself. Yet, as we will
see, this solution has been severely undermined by social transformations that have occurred in the past 30 years.

A Theory of Justice by John Rawls (1971) can rightfully be considered as the manifesto of the liberal political theory of the second half of the twentieth century. The period during which the book was conceived is hallmarked by two main trends, which are relevant from both a theoretical-cultural and a social-political perspective: 1) the revival of practical philosophy (moral and political), partly as a reaction to the waning of utilitarianism as the dominant paradigm in the normative field; and 2) the epoch-making development of the welfare state (mostly in Europe), which was meant to be a third way between the public policies defended by classical liberalism and the harsh criticisms raised against them from Marxist positions. Although the text is explicitly conceived as a work of moral philosophy (and not primarily as a text pertaining to legal or political theory), based on an original form of contractualism formulated in Kantian terms, the theory of justice as fairness advanced by Rawls may be nonetheless conceived as a praise of the welfare state as it was developed in the last century. Within this perspective, *A Theory of Justice* defends a model of political constitution that is able to combine needs for stability and demands for social justice within a firm and consistent constitutional framework.

To the basic question of how to guarantee a political constitution and establish social and economic conditions based on fairness – that is, shaped in such a way as to be ideally accepted by free and equal individuals in an initial condition wherein no information on one's own social position is available – Rawls provides the following response: justice as fairness requires that basic or primary social goods (that is, those goods that prove to be necessary for any personal project of life, whatever it may be) must be equally distributed unless an unequal distribution is to the greatest benefit of the least advantaged. Within this perspective, justice consists in the enactment of universal normative principles that can be accepted by rational actors who are mutually disinterested and willing to cooperate with each other, that is, by individuals who deliberate by removing from consideration the particular role and status they have in their family, social and national context.

This general conception is based on two principles of justice, lexicographically ordered (in the sense that the requirements of the second must be subordinated to the conditions set by the first). The first principle states that each person has an equal right to the most extensive basic liberties compatible with a similar liberty for others. The second principle states that, in order to be accepted as legitimate, a given inequality must be the outcome of a fair competition, in which the same opportunities for success are concretely guaranteed for every competitor (*a*), and must achieve a substantial improvement of the absolute conditions of the least advantaged (*b*).

After more than 20 years, however, Rawls radically revised his theory of justice. In *Political Liberalism* (Rawls 1993) he reassesses both the methodological approach and the normative outcome characterizing *A Theory of Justice*. In his second book, Rawls argues that the theory advanced in his previous work is seriously flawed in that it assumes the conception of *justice as fairness* as a universal moral ideal that is expected to be accepted by every rational agent in any historical and cultural context because of its being impartial and equidistant from the various and conflicting ethical perspectives that are present in society. According to Rawls, this Kantian perspective can no longer be considered as a neutral 'view from nowhere': justice as fairness is in its turn a particular 'view of the world' like any other and, as such, it is called upon to *publicly* justify its assumptions within a social context in which different individuals support different 'conceptions of the good', which are only partially compatible with each other.

In *Political Liberalism* the question of justice is closely related to that of stability: in contemporary societies politics has the primary task of dealing with the 'fact of pluralism', that is, the inevitable and constitutive presence of a plurality of different views of the world, which Rawls terms 'comprehensive doctrines'. Accordingly, the basic question of liberalism becomes the following: since a society in which all members endorse a unique view of the world, such as the one advanced in *A Theory of Justice*, is neither realistic nor desirable, is there a political system able to ensure the peaceful coexistence of the various comprehensive doctrines while preserving their essential diversity?

The answer offered by Rawls is based on a conception of justice that he defines as *political*, in that it is grounded in an *overlapping consensus* and justified on the basis of the idea of *public reason*. The concepts highlighted in italics are key to Rawls's theory and need to be considered in more detail.

A conception of justice is political – where 'political' is indeed synonymous with 'constitutional' – if it proves to be actually independent of any metaphysical, epistemological and even moral assumption: individuals are expected to perceive themselves no longer as moral agents, but, in a less ambitious vein, as democratic citizens who identify themselves in a fundamental constitution and in liberal institutions, independent of any other extra-political principle or belief. What is more, these non-political assumptions must be completely excluded from the public debate on political institutions because they are not (and, presumably, cannot be) shared by all citizens.

If citizens are *reasonable*, an 'overlapping consensus' is not only possible but also the best available solution. Citizens are reasonable if they recognize and accept that the different comprehensive doctrines characterizing a given context are equally legitimate even if mutually irreducible, and are nonetheless willing to cooperate with each other under equal conditions that can be accepted by all. On the contrary, unreasonable are those who wish to impose as binding for all, the social rules and lifestyle that hallmark their own particular comprehensive doctrine. The overlapping consensus essentially consists in finding a minimum core of normative principles and political arrangements that is actually shared or ideally acceptable by all: that is, a public ground for deliberation (in essence, a shared constitutional framework) that can be endorsed by all reasonable comprehensive doctrines. This political solution is made possible by the fact that every reasonable doctrine already contains values and reasons that, although in different forms and with a variety of different aims from doctrine to doctrine, are sufficient to account for and substantiate the political principles that ground the conception of justice as fairness. In a nutshell, every reasonable comprehensive doctrine – although for different reasons, which probably would not be accepted outside of the ethical and cultural context that considers them as binding – actually agrees on a minimum set of rules for the coexistence of very different social groups that would otherwise be doomed to violent conflict.

In other words, an epistemological filter is an essential precondition for public reasoning: the only reasons that can be legitimately advanced in the political realm are those that are actually already shared by all reasonable doctrines that are present in a liberal and democratic social context. Within this perspective, the more an argument (and the principles that follow from it) is shared by a larger number of comprehensive doctrines, the more it is reasonable. It should be noted, by the way, that more often than not 'comprehensive doctrines' ends up being an umbrella term for a motley array of far more complex and even contradictory cultural features and social trends that characterize a given political context, which Rawls tends to approach in a very reductionist way.

Beyond any other consideration on the relevance and consistency of Rawls's arguments, what is to be emphasized for present purposes is that the transition from *A Theory of Justice* to *Political Liberalism* can be considered the theoretical translation of both the historical path of liberalism and the profound differences between the historical and political contexts that separate the two works.

According to this interpretation, *A Theory of Justice* represents, as we have said above, the philosophical manifesto of the welfare state, which saw its greatest expansion and efficiency in the early 1970s. The quarter of a century that separates Rawls's *magnum opus* from the end of World War II was characterized by social and economic trends that paved the way to the golden age of welfare: unprecedented rates of economic growth, high wages, low inflation and an epoch-making improvement of social welfare (both Europe and the United States are currently facing a profound economic contraction of all these indexes coupled with a major crisis of confidence). Until the last quarter of the last century, the key role of the state was uncontested and undisputed: the state is the guarantor of fair economic and social conditions, that is, the provider, allocator and regulator of goods and opportunities that must be equally distributed to all individuals, in such a way as to reduce, if not eliminate, the social disparities that exist among citizens.

Within this perspective, the *capabilities approach* mainly developed by the Indian economist Amartya Sen (1992, 2009) can be considered, more than other more political theories, the most interesting critical revision and further development of the inclusive and egalitarian project of a fair distribution of primary goods carried out by Rawls. In particular, Sen argues that a fair theory of distributive justice must take into due consideration the individual differences in the ability to transform the essential resources and primary goods allocated into concrete possibilities of realizing one's own goals and improving one's own living conditions. The basic conditions are different because they are structurally dependent on the individual resources available (which vary from person to person) and the particular context of action.

On the other hand, the historical framework in which *Political Liberalism* is rooted appears to be profoundly different from the previous one. The implosion of the Soviet system and the consequences of the different processes of decolonization and independence that took place in postcolonial contexts on the one hand, and the impact of the energy crises that marked the final decades of the last century coupled with some structural changes in the capitalist economy on the other, determined the crisis of the previous political model. At the end of the century, liberalism faces attacks on two fronts: it has to counter both the radical reaction of the neo-liberal ideology in the early 1980s and the ethnical and identitarian claims put forward by political communities and minorities that can no longer be managed through the normative tools provided by the traditional state-centred perspective. As a consequence, liberal theory is forced to open up to demands of recognition made by various collective entities and to capitalize on the legacy of rival traditions (above all, communitarianism). In sum, liberalism is forced to acknowledge the irreducible plurality of approaches and views of the world that do not appear to be compatible.

The reference model now becomes a state whose essential task is to ensure the preservation of a minimal consensus for the resolution of possible disagreements or conflicts among members of groups with different identities, needs and traditions, especially with regard to the very question of what are the duties and functions that a state has to perform. As a result, the political task that state institutions seek to accomplish, by mediating between immutable universal principles and irreducible cultural differences (Ferrara 1999; Forst 2002), becomes more and more demanding and ultimately hopeless.

The transition period between the first and the second model of state – that is, from the state as a guarantor of fair social and economic conditions to the state as a mediator between radically different social groups and communities – is marked by what has been defined as the 'contextual turn' of contemporary political theory. Notably, an ever-increasing attention is paid to the local political contexts, characterized by different public affairs, approached in different ways as a response to different needs. A first serious attempt to extend the analysis to the contextual conditions of redistributive policies has been made, as we have said above, by Amartya Sen with the capabilities approach. Yet, the political and philosophical debate of the last two decades of the last century, at least as far as the debate between universalism and contextualism is concerned, has been marked by the various criticisms raised by a well-defined group of different theorists, usually defined as 'communitarians'.

According to *communitarianism*, communitarian contexts and relations (family, neighbourhood, associations, political groups and so on) represent practical as well as social preconditions for the development of personal identity. Within this perspective, the particular needs of such contexts of interaction should therefore be acknowledged and satisfied even in a liberal perspective. Liberalism, on the other hand, tends to completely disregard – at least according to its critics – any form of contextual social bonds and to replace them with pre-social forms of contractualism, which prove to be, in the last instance, unrealistic and misleading abstractions. (Obviously the same criticism can be levelled at the 'imagined' communities described and defended by most communitarians: Anderson 2006.) According to one of the most relevant communitarian criticisms, the concept of neutrality, which lies at the heart of the liberal proposal, is but an ideological construction that is based on a specific and particular (although not explicit) conception of the good. (As we have seen above, this criticism has been accepted, at least in part, by Rawls himself.) According to communitarianism, then, justice consists in the preservation of the highest common good represented by the particular lifestyle that is shared by all the members of a communitarian context, who identify themselves as belonging to a given ethical and cultural tradition.

Michael Walzer can be considered the first theorist who has trans-lated into theoretical and philosophical terms the paradigm shift that was then taking place in the social and political realm. This is particularly relevant to our analysis because Walzer's fundamental aim is that of mediating between liberal positions and communitarian criticisms. This is why Walzer has distanced himself from other and more radical versions of communitarianism, such as those put forward by Alasdair MacIntyre (2007), Charles Taylor (1989) and Michael Sandel (1998).

Spheres of Justice (Walzer 1983) is but a radical methodological critique of any abstract distributive paradigm that claims to be able to apply to any historical and social context. Walzer's basic argument is comprised of two distinct tenets: 1) a theory of justice that is grounded on a *single and allegedly rational distributive paradigm*, based on a *single decision-making* centre, meant to allocate a *single set of fundamental goods*, according to a *single criterion of justice*, represents a potentially totalitarian imposition to the irreducible plurality of the different cultural and social contexts (from both a historical and a spatial perspective); 2) there exist as many fully legitimate distributive paradigms, decision-making processes, sets of fundamental goods, criteria of justice as there are communitarian contexts (past, present and future) in which the different conceptions of the goods are shaped and on which they are essentially dependent from both an epistemological and a practical standpoint.

In particular, any communitarian context is comprised of a plurality of more or less extensive social spheres, that is, differentiated spaces of interaction and distribution. Every sphere is ruled by a different principle of distribution, according to the particular good that is shaped, developed and allocated within it. Within this perspective, according to which every sphere is characterized by different models of interaction among members and resolution of social conflicts, the state is only one of the various providers of goods (the largest part of which is developed in non-public contexts). The challenge is how to bring these different contexts of social interaction together so as to safeguard the different goods they provide. According to Walzer, therefore, justice consists in distributing the different social goods according to the specific criteria for allocation that can be deduced by the social meanings attributed to each good and shared by all members within a given communitarian context.

After having defended and supported such a pluralization of the communitarian contexts and the social spaces for sharing and distributing the different social goods, Walzer (1997) relies on the various forms of toleration that have historically been adopted in different contexts to settle the inevitable conflicts among groups, both internal and external to the state. As Walzer himself emphasizes, toleration makes difference possible, difference makes toleration necessary. Within this perspective, what legitimates a regime of toleration – that is, a firm guarantee of the preservation of the main different forms of social interaction within a given community – is simply the basic fact that it is actually able to perpetuate the coexistence between potentially conflicting groups, independent of the reasons that the various groups may advance to account for their positions. As in the case of Rawls's *Political Liberalism*, then, the shift from an individualist approach to a group-centred perspective lowers the ambitions in terms of normative justification in favour of a recognition of the political practices that are actually adopted and established in a given context, provided that they comply with minimum conditions for the resolution of conflicts (and, more often than not, avoiding violence is considered as a sufficient condition for legitimation).

The strategy in question refers to a historical horizon marked by what are, according to Walzer, the two fundamental changes, strictly interrelated, that occurred in recent years.

From a historical and political standpoint, the process of the formation of political unity is profoundly changed. Until the early 1970s independence movements, mostly in Europe, aimed at achieving (national) statehood so as to assimilate and unify divided peoples, embedded in centuries-old empires or fragmented into a plurality of small principalities; since the last quarter of the twentieth century, minority groups no longer demand to be assimilated into a larger political entity but, quite the contrary, pursue recognition for the group as a different and autonomous community.

From a practical and normative standpoint, the first modern project of toleration has been replaced by the second one. The first project – which concerned the conflicts among individuals, between individuals and groups, and among groups – was based on the politics of progressive democratic inclusion: Jews, workers, women, blacks, immigrants and other discriminated subjects organized themselves into movements, parties and associations in order to voice their claims in the political field as excluded minorities and to gain recognition as individuals who deserve fair and equal treatment like any other citizen. The second modern project of toleration – which concerns the conflicts between the groups and the state and mainly between the state and the identitarian communities (which Walzer terms 'tribes') – is based on deep-rooted politics of communitarian division. The aim is no longer a common and equal inclusion of discriminated individuals, but to separate the groups with the aim of preserving their difference, by granting them a more or less large degree of self-rule and autonomy (within a range that goes from devolution to independence).

In such a perspective, the main task of both normative reflection and political field is that – indeed very limited – of recognizing (and to a certain extent supporting) the spread of ethical, historical and cultural differences, by seeking to settle, whenever possible, the conflicts arising between groups. The main political task, therefore, according to this proposal, is to expand and strengthen the space of autonomy that has to be reserved not only for individuals, but first and foremost for the social spheres, communitarian contexts and collective entities with which individuals identify in a more intimate and immediate way than they might have in the more articulated, anonymous and depersonalizing state dimension.

By adopting an approach more responsive to normative requirements, Will Kymlicka has put forward a multicultural version of both the liberal theory and distributive paradigm – different from radical multiculturalism, which intends to get rid of the theory and paradigm in question (see 3.1.1) – according to which the minority groups internal to the state have the right to receive certain social goods and a given amount of power in order to enable them to perpetuate themselves as distinct and autonomous cultural contexts. Within this perspective, only through such a political recognition can the members of the different minority groups actually realize their own projects, by pursuing their particular ideal of a good life. Also in this case, the basic assumption – again in stark contrast to the traditional conception of liberal neutrality – is that cultural and religious differences, far from being irrelevant in the public sphere, constitute the fundamental diversity that the state is called upon to recognize and preserve from both a pragmatic and a normative viewpoint.

Indeed, the relevance of difference as a political cornerstone must be recognized not only in the public sphere, but first and foremost at the level of normative justification and actual organization of differentiated public policies. Treating citizens equally does not mean treating them as equal, since there are minority groups that have no or little ability to influence the policies pursued by the majority as their *essential* diversity and fundamental identity *systematically* prevent them from becoming a majority. To remedy this situation, the state legal order can (and should) introduce exceptions for some groups and not for others; institutions also can (and should) reserve more resources to the groups whose cultural legacy is threatened by dispersion, re-assimilation or even extinction. Hence a series of measures is introduced both to concretely include these minority groups in the public debate and to grant them social spaces to realize, and in so doing perpetuate, the models of life present in their culture: among these measures are territorial autonomy, veto powers, quotas for representation, local exemptions and linguistic rights.

In a book tellingly titled *Multicultural Citizenship*, Kymlicka (1995) first makes a distinction between *multinational states* and *polyethnic states*. In the first case cultural difference originates from the assimilation of once-autonomous cultural groups concentrated in a defined territory. In the second, cultural difference is a major consequence of the different waves of immigration of individuals and families that had occurred. After making a further distinction between *self-government rights* and *polyethnic rights* (financial support and legal protection for given practices adopted by ethnic and religious groups) and *social representation rights*, Kymlicka deals with the question of the compatibility between individual autonomy and communitarian culture. In doing so, he makes a final distinction between two kinds of collective rights: 'internal restrictions' enable the group to restrict the liberty of individual members in the name of group solidarity or cultural integrity; 'external protections', instead, enable the larger community to protect the endangered groups from the economic or political pressure exerted by external groups or society, in order to prevent minority necessities being overridden by majority decisions.

Without denying that a peaceful society is doomed to remain an illusion, the second kind of collective rights proves to be not only compatible with the demands of liberal autonomy, but also a vital integration of them.

More recently, Kymlicka (2007) has provided a comprehensive analysis of what he considers as a second and relevant wave of the multicultural trend. It consists essentially in an ever-increasing and explicit recognition of the prerogatives and rights of various minorities by the international community, as to both its legal resolutions and the policies carried out by its institutional or extra-institutional organs (support, advice, funds and so on). As a result, the different relations between the state and the various ethnic groups, until then confined to the national horizon of citizenship, have gained an unprecedented and growing international relevance. Multicultural politics appears thus to be 'a morally progressive extension of existing human rights norms' (Kymlicka 2007: 7), in particular with regard to three distinct social groups: indigenous peoples, national minorities and immigrants.

Yet, the global extension of the multicultural model has to deal with the fact that 'multiculturalism is a liberal-democratic phenomenon' (Kymlicka 2007: 97). As such, it depends on historical and political conditions that are actually linked to both a common legal and normative framework, which is not yet established at a global level, and historical contingencies that have no discernible effect on the current situation.

In fact, multicultural claims are the ultimate outcome of specific and circumscribed historical factors, above all: the awareness of one's own rights, the demographic growth of minority groups, the consolidation of democratic regimes within which demands of recognition can be advanced, the Western legal legacy in post-colonial contexts and a certain confidence in the conduct of the international community. In turn, the recognition of these claims by state and non-state institutions has been widely supported by two further elements: the almost unanimous consent on the very human rights whose enforcement greatly contributed to reducing recurrent internal conflicts (by giving priority to human rights over cultural rights in any case); and the process of desecuritization, that is, the end of the bipolar world (USA vs. USSR), within which any form of recognition of some degree of autonomy would have entailed the unacceptable risk that the autonomous territory would fall under the influence of the enemy.

Presently these two basic conditions are at risk. On the one hand, the consent on human rights is no longer an unquestioned cornerstone of international politics or a common and unquestioned basis for discussion; on the other hand, the international community as such appears to be less protected from both internal and external violent forms of fundamentalism and integralism (as is proved also by the immigration policies adopted by the US and the EU, especially in the case of Muslims in the so-called 'war on terrorism'). According to Kymlicka, a yet more decisive and radical multicultural policy by the international community would be able not only to reduce these risks but also to pave the way to more comprehensive measures based on an effective human rights system, by ensuring a peaceful settlement of conflicts and supporting a wider democratic inclusion.

Lastly, 'weak' liberalism put forward by Richard Rorty (1989) can be considered the final stage of development of the 'liberal century'. For the first time, the universalistic claims underlying liberal principles are openly criticized not only from outside liberal tradition, but also from perspectives that are internal to it and in the name of its own values. As a result, the rationalist and universalist project carried out by modern liberalism is reduced to, among other things, a contingent cultural tradition characteristic of a given geo-historical context and, as such, is inconceivable to other traditions. Within this perspective, exporting liberalism in a non-liberal context is (or at least risks being) just an unjustifiable form of ideological and political imperialism. Accordingly, Rorty suggests an *ironic liberalism*, that is, a disenchanted attitude according to which a liberal attitude, by recognizing the incommensurability of different cultural traditions, has to give up its original unattainable and sinister goals and to pursue only the essential aim of replacing violent imposition with persuasion, in the hope that social suffering can be reduced as much as possible by supporting forms of sympathetic solidarity. To achieve this non-rationalist aim, a captivating fictional narrative is more suitable than abstract philosophical arguments.

1.1.2 Metamorphoses of government

In the previous section, the shift from a political theory grounded in the concept of the individual to a theory based on the plurality of groups allowed us to consider how the *subject of politics* changes. In this section, the analysis will focus on similar changes to the *object of government*, that is, its fields of action, its strategies of intervention and its fundamental goals.

To analyze this second evolution in more detail, we will deal with two political theories that have paid special attention to the issue of government: republicanism and the biopolitical paradigm. Indeed, despite being very different in both basic assumptions and theoretical aims, both the theories discuss extensively, although from opposite perspectives, the concept of *domination*. In the first case, domination consists in a *condition of dependence that mostly occurs in the absence of government*. Government, in its turn, is conceived of as *the articulation of the constitutional whole and the endogenous factor for ensuring a stable balance of power*. In the second case, instead, domination refers to a *technique of subjectification that mostly occurs in the presence of government*. In a nutshell, subjectification consists in the creation and imposition of new subjectivities and new models of action, which reflect and support the dominant social imperatives. Government, in its turn, consists in *an actual orientation and implementation of a specific plan of action*.

Republicanism – also termed 'neo-republicanism' (Honohan 2002) to distinguish it from classical republicanism, or 'civil republicanism' (Maynor 2003) to distinguish it from constitutional republicanism – initially emerged as a 'third voice' in the debate between liberals and communitarians. The basic aim of republicans is not mediation between the two conflicting positions but rather overcoming them, so as to establish a political community within which liberal provisions can be complemented by civic bonds able to encourage and increase what is currently a more and more discouraged and limited participation of citizens in the democratic process.

Republicanism is a political theory that considers a specific kind of freedom, i.e. *freedom as non-domination or independence from arbitrary power* (be it personal or institutional), as the highest value that should lie at the heart of any political association. A power is arbitrary whenever it is not limited externally by norms, procedures or goals known to the individuals and groups involved. Any association hallmarked by the absence of domination can be defined as a republic, that is, a community in which every citizen is sovereign and which is thus based on both equal rights for everyone and the common good (that is, a good that cannot be increased or decreased for one person without thereby increasing or decreasing it for everyone: this is the case, for example, with freedom of thought and with knowledge itself). What is peculiar to republicanism is the emphasis that is placed on this concept of *res publica*: government must never be conceived as the exclusive property of someone, but always as a mutual sharing of equal rights and responsibilities, carried out in the interest of all citizens in compliance with what they consider to be their interest.

The advocates of republicanism explicitly distinguish freedom as non-domination from the *negative freedom* that hallmarks most liberal theories. While according to this latter conception we are free if and only if our plans of action do not suffer interference from some external factor (freedom as *non-interference*), according to republicanism we are free if and only if our action plans are completely independent from some external will (freedom as *non-dependence*). An example that is often used in the critical literature can help us understand what it means to say that domination can occur without interference. A group of slaves has the good fortune to depend on a benevolent and non-interfering master, who leaves them free to act as they wish, although he has a right of life and death over them. Can these slaves be considered free? The advocates of republicanism argue that a narrow conception of freedom, such as the liberal one, would inevitably lead to an affirmative answer.

In contrast, republicans argue that true political freedom can be seen only in the absence of any form of arbitrary domination. In other words, freedom should not be the contingent outcome of unstable situations, but a mutual relationship aimed at ensuring the rights of everyone: we are dominated not only whenever a concrete act of dominance is being carried out, but also whenever there is the *constant and lasting possibility* of such an outcome. With regard to this issue, Philip Pettit, the most prominent neo-republican theorist, has recently argued that an ongoing *control exercised by others* should be considered a sufficient condition for there being domination.

Freedom as non-domination is introduced as a third way with regard to the traditional opposition between negative liberty (freedom *from*) and positive liberty (freedom *of*). Roughly speaking, while liberal freedom consists in the absence of interference and democratic freedom in self-government, republican freedom consists in a constitutional guarantee against any form of mastery. From the republican viewpoint, then, liberal freedom proves insufficient (as seen, we can be dominated even if no one has ever interfered with our plans of action) and democratic freedom unnecessary (we can be free – that is, not subject to the whim of others – without thereby being masters of ourselves).

In concrete terms, freedom as non-domination emphasizes the fact that no person can be said to be free if she is forced to live with the fear that she might suffer a serious injustice or a profound humiliation and with the overwhelming temptation to please the powerful, the immediate consequence of which is an unconscious tendency to self-censorship. Obviously, in such a condition it is very easy to lose one's self-esteem and the esteem of others. The enactment of a consistent set of non-arbitrary rules – that is, abstract, general and aimed at the common good – is the best way to provide for a political system that can actually ensure the freedom of all. The highest freedom can thus be achieved only in a republican regime within which citizens are equally subject to the rule of law and there exist neither masters nor slaves.

What must be emphasized is that, from a republican viewpoint, the democratic law is a paradigmatic case of interference without domination, that is, the opposite case to that considered above of domination without interference. Although the constraints, restrictions and penalties imposed by the law undoubtedly interfere with one's projects, they cannot be considered forms of arbitrary power. Indeed, they are not direct or personal orders given by someone to someone else in an asymmetrical and unidirectional relationship, but indirect and impersonal orders given by every citizen to every other in a peer-to-peer and mutual relationship.

However, what ultimately distinguishes republicanism is not primarily the concept of freedom it introduces, but rather the civic and institutional conditions that are considered necessary for the preservation and enjoyment of the freedom at stake. There are two main groups of conditions, both aimed at preventing and limiting as much as possible the development of any form of domination: from a legal and institutional viewpoint, the constitutional framework meant as an essential limitation, division and mutual check of state powers (Bellamy 2007); and from an ethical and political viewpoint, the civic or public virtue (Dagger 1997).

Constitutional guarantees are divided into filters (or preventive procedures) and sanctions (or punitive procedures). The former are meant to define and limit the range of legitimate actions, by establishing that only certain actors are authorized and only certain actions are permitted. The latter are intended to discourage any act that is detrimental to the freedom and well-being of others, by punishing the wrongdoers. Yet, these measures may not be sufficient to avoid what has been defined as the 'rule of persons' replacing the rule of law. In this regard, by assuming that what makes a given course of action arbitrary is not so much the lack of consent but the lack of the possibility of contesting such a decision in an effective way, *contestability* is the other pillar of republican constitutionalism: republican institutions must shape a deliberative, inclusive and responsive democracy. Concretely this means that any political deliberation must be open to (argumentative) contestation and consequently that adequate procedures and spaces to articulate, discuss and reply to contestations must be provided.

Public or civic virtue is the real driving force and lifeblood of any republican community. Without it, it is much harder for citizens to feel they are part of a common project and for constitutional engineering to fulfil its functions of guarantee and control. Civic virtue essentially consists in being willing to put aside personal interests (even if legitimate) whenever it is of substantial advantage to the common good. The fundamental function of the public virtue is thus to 'transform' statutory law – which in turn is called upon to adequately meet the needs of civil society – into socially shared and generally observed rules, so that both set of norms can support one another.

Both early and most recent accounts of republicanism (see, respectively, Pettit 1997; Lovett 2010) are founded on the same concept of domination (a major aim pursued by the most recent versions of republicanism is that of accounting for a more consistent, effective and fair concept of public intervention). It refers to a condition experienced by individuals or groups who are actually dependent on a social context in which other persons or groups willingly exercise an arbitrary power, which is intended to be detrimental to the condition of the former. From which it follows that domination consists exclusively in interactions between individuals or groups of individuals and it is possible only in the presence of a clear intention of damaging the targets of these arbitrary measures.

Given these essential features, there is no relevant form of domination that cannot be approached and tackled within the state framework and through the legal and political resources that are available to public institutions, as the examples made in the critical literature on republicanism also clearly demonstrate (slavery, discrimination of minorities, colonial policies, exploitative relationships, family abuses). Within this perspective, then, the more a society provides for and preserves social contexts free of domination, by extending their spaces and supporting their tasks, the more it is just. Finally, this process of communitarian or collective emancipation must be carried out primarily by government and public institutions in general, in compliance with the limits set by the constitution.

The starting point of the *biopolitical paradigm* can be identified in a complete reversal of the republican approach. Government is no longer concerned with the eradication of the conditions that make domination possible in order to achieve a given ideal of justice (which is now conceived, on the contrary, as a mere ideological device for domination and control). Rather, it deals with *techniques of subjectification* aimed at shaping the field of social action within which individuals structure their personality, interact and relate to one another – that is, in the words of Foucault, 'to conduct the conducts'. Accordingly, power is no longer conceived as a mere form of (or source for) repression, but in a more ambivalent and complex perspective, as a productive and creative instance that shapes new models of conduct and new patterns of action.

Also in this case, as in that of liberalism, state as both a framework and a political actor loses its centrality. The state, as a guarantor of social spaces free from domination, becomes an ordering institution among others in a comprehensive network of techniques and logics of power that partially overcome and partially rely on it. Accordingly, individuals are no longer conceived as being limited in their options by some interference, as argued by republicans, but, more radically, as the ultimate outcome of the motley array of perspectives and models of life that prevail in a given social context. Although the key issues addressed by the biopolitical paradigm appear to be the same as the political theories that have marked the modern era (well-being, security, independence, conflict and so on), they are actually debated from a very different perspective, according to which governmental action imposes itself as a super-personal and anonymous activity that is presented to the governed, in a confidence-inspiring and paternal way, as an essential precondition for their own self-fulfilment.

Biopolitics literally means 'government of life'. More exactly, the concept refers to the various techniques of government and forms of power that focus on individuals as living beings, that is, ultimately, as a biological body. To mention just a few: public health measures, anti-terrorism programmes, the big data system, bioethical guidelines, the control of the territory through GPS devices and the legal regulation of sexual relations are all examples of biopolitical strategies that decisively contribute to orient, influence and affect both our life and our personality. The biopolitical policies are based on two main pillars: on the one hand, the enforcement of extremely intrusive and indefinitely protracted measures of preventive security; and on the other hand, the legitimacy of an unlimited extension of emergency legislation (Bazzicalupo 2010; Plant 2010).

Originally developed as a historical and interpretive paradigm by Michel Foucault mostly in the lectures hold at the *Collège de France* in the years 1977–9, biopolitics focuses on two strictly intertwined phenomena, which complement each other and lead to what Foucault has defined the 'state control of the biological'. They are, respectively: *Security, Territory, Population* and *The Birth of Biopolitics* (Foucault 2007, 2008; Lemke 1997 – for the legal and political relevance of Foucault's approach, see respectively Golden and Fitzpatrick 2009; Dillon and Neal 2008). On the one hand, political action aims more and more at the determination, regulation and organization of the

constitutive stages and the basic needs that mark the life of the
population of a given territory; on the other hand, individuals are the
first to urge the government to plan, ensure and supervise every stage
of their own existence.

Any resource and strategy that proves to be functional in the
preservation and prolongation of life is thus maximized by implementing policies based on the security of individuals (security
devices) and the preservation of social environments from any source
of risk and any foreign body (immunization policies). The immediate
consequence is that politics and human life determine and modify
each other: the more biopower moulds human life, by reassessing
its basic features and ranking its fundamental needs through the
management of the main resources and vital forces of a population,
the more the biological existence of the individual affects such a
power, by influencing, in turn, its basic aims and its logic of legitimation, which actually consists in just ensuring specific standards of
efficiency without resorting to (direct) violence.

In the biopolitical perspective, the paradigm of modern sovereignty turns out to be but an ideological device unable to grasp
reality. As such, it should be replaced by a more articulated analysis of
the different and even contradictory ways in which power is exercised
(Esposito 2008). In particular, there is no longer any legal and institutional mediation between the public sphere, in which political
power is exercised, and the private sphere, which mainly concerns
the body and the biological life of individuals, and the production of
goods and reproduction of the self. This is particularly evident in the
contraposition between the artificial and constructed order imposed
by the state and the natural and spontaneous order created by society
(Agamben 1998). Obligation and coercion – the two pillars of the
vertical and binding relationship between sovereign and subjects
that hallmarked the mainstream legal and political philosophy of
the modern era – are thus replaced by a political system and logic of

government aimed at directly empowering individuals by assuring them a substantial degree of discretion within a well-defined interactional context.

From this perspective, life is no longer depicted as a prior condition for and an indirect target of governmental action, which is beyond politics, but as both something that must be created, moulded, shaped (function of subjectification) and the primary target of the political (function of subjection). To achieve these basic aims, the contingency and precariousness of human life, which is at once served by and put at the service of the sovereign forces of social development, must be controlled and rationalized. To use Foucault's famous formulation, the sovereign right to 'make die and let live' is replaced by the power to 'make live and let die'.

This paradigm shift inevitably brings about a radical change in the way government is conceived. According to this reassessment, governmental action comprises two main strategies: *governance* and *governmentality*.

Governance refers to the set of practices, activities and policies – not necessarily related to formal procedures or legal responsibility, as in the case of government – that decisively contribute to developing a common and multilevel strategy adopted by various and unrelated social actors to achieve a given goal (which is shared in different forms and with different aims). Specific governance, then, allows cooperatively combining and meeting the demands of different individuals and institutions (both public and private) by pursuing a common goal and imposing (mostly) informal rules of conduct. In this way, this strategy is able to influence, replace and even determine public policies whenever public institutions prove to be unable or unwilling, for whatever reason, to autonomously achieve their aims.

The concept of *governmentality* refers to the technique of government that hallmarks the biopolitical paradigm. It essentially consists in a critical account of the way in which problems of governance are approached and solved (above all, how to establish and maintain uniform patterns of behaviour and reliable standards of conduct). The choice of the term 'governmentality' is meant to emphasize the priority of the governmental power – that is, the substantial amount of power that is available to the government – over the others (in particular, over disciplining and sovereign power). In the words of Foucault, governance consists in 'the ensemble formed by institutions, procedures, analyses and reflections, calculations and tactics that allow the exercise of this very specific, albeit very complex, power that has the population as its target, political economy as its major form of knowledge, and apparatuses of security as its essential technical instrument' (Foucault 2007: 108).

According to the biopolitical paradigm – and the underlying genealogy that links classical liberalism and the different models of welfare state developed in the last century to the current age of neo-liberalism (Harvey 2005) – what we usually label as 'power' should not be conceived as something *held* by a legal and political centre, but as something *emanating* via a complex web of decentralized and overlapping technologies of supervision. Governmental politics has one fundamental aim: the manipulation and technical reproduction of what, according to our self-understanding as human beings, makes humans human. In pursuing this aim, the experts and specialists in a particular field (officials, bureaucrats, consultants, professionals) are the agents of the enterprise; the establishment of a network of standard benchmarks, adopted to rank the spreading capabilities of the individuals, constitutes the task; the implementation of a set of orienting practices and corrective strategies (ordering, discipline, rehabilitation), meant to trace the right track and redirect those who go for the bad, represents the means adopted to achieve the basic aim.

What lies at the heart of the biopolitical paradigm is thus a far-reaching social programme based on statistical forecasts and management strategies aimed at accounting for, and reducing the complexity of, fluid ties and ever-changing relationships that lead to innovative forms of interactions between actors and practices, power and knowledge, spheres and domains. The common ground of economical measurability, calculability and predictability is what permits both the interactional process among competing individuals and an effective control over them. Within this perspective, the political as such is reduced to a relationship between costs and benefits, which essentially aims at maximizing competitiveness and efficiency. The ultimate task of the biopower is thus to be viewed in the enforcement of a complex set of policies aimed at increasing and empowering the skills and capabilities of every social actor (individuals, families, markets, states), in order to promote those attitudes, behaviours and activities that prove to be beneficial for the preservation of the free market as the driving force and the immanent rationality of the system as a whole. Accordingly, by shaping a political programme based on the actual self-government of society, the biopower finds its legitimacy in the minimization of risks and the maximization of well-being at both an individual and a collective level.

The new forms of management sketched above actually escape the net of legal regulation, even in the case of a transnational set of norms. As a result, a relevant part of the legal sphere, as well as the very concept of political accountability as such, becomes an empty shell. In order to foster and promote personal well-being in ways that are functional to the perpetuation of determinate models of conduct and forms of subjectification, government exercises a complete control over the different phases of the biological life of individuals. Personal security and the preservation of the social environment from any sources of risk are the political preconditions to the 'creation' of docile bodies best suited to comply with the pragmatic conditions required or imposed by the system. These strategies are part of a larger group of technologies of power – that is, ways to produce certain desired effects within a given interactional context – that induce individuals to conceive of consumerism as the best way to self-realization. This leads to what has been termed 'identity through consumption', a process that turns citizens into *sovereign consumers who choose among a number of different providers*: individuals are depicted as self-interested and enterprising agents that (are forced to) act – that is, make their own choices and take their own risks – in a highly competitive society.

This attempt to reduce society to the market provides, imposes and recognizes only one model of well-ordered society, conceived for a well-defined model of autonomous agent which is called upon to self-govern. As a consequence, any lifestyle or subject that appears to be incompatible with the high-performing standards required by the system is marginalized, that is, pushed to the margins of society as a subversive element and rendered socially invisible. The political conflict, in its different forms and degrees, is replaced by permanent and informal negotiation, grounded in the binary code beneficial– unbeneficial and aimed at the most effective management of all the resources available. It is no longer a normative code that determines a given outcome, but is the outcome to be reached that determines the normative framework. This dislocation of power, which radically undermines any kind of formal responsibilities and procedures of control, is thus grounded in a rigid and unquestionable definition of what is normal, consistent and acceptable and what is not.

Although the primary aim of the different interpretations carried out by the advocates of the biopolitical paradigm is to emphasize the radical change in the way government is conceived and managed, another and no less important aim (whether overtly expressed or not and pursued with more or less consistency) is to be viewed in the critical attitude held by all these authors towards the metamorphosis they are describing. In particular, they argue that the new forms of government, which are more often than not ideologically presented as both a natural evolution and an inescapable fate, inevitably lead to a dramatic and generalized loss of freedom, both individual and collective.

According to this criticism, the biopower, by reducing normative validity to standards of effectiveness and functionality, breaks the social whole into different and monadic parts, which are in turn forced to adapt to a totalizing way of life. The security and assistance guaranteed by the governmental state ends up turning citizens into addicted clients, whose well-being essentially depends on the amount of services and commodities provided by the market. As a result, the preservation of life is placed into the hands of those same powers and agents that, by also relying on this confidence, pursue aims that actually prevent both the empowerment of individuals and the full development of personal identity. *Thanatopolitics* (repression in the name of survival) and *démocrature* (control in exchange for security) are the terms coined to describe these degenerate forms of the governmental paradigm, along with the reference – in our opinion conceptually misleading – to the concept of *empire*, introduced to refer to what is depicted as an aggressive and uncontrolled expansion on a global scale of a polycentric society of control (Hardt and Negri 2000).

1.1.3 The legacy of the constitution

Starting from the end of World War II, three main changes have been occurring in constitutional jurisprudence and, more generally, in the way constitution as the legal structure of the state is conceived. First, the enforcement of rigid constitutions, that is, constitutions that contain norms that cannot be modified (let alone replaced) by the same organs and procedures adopted to enact ordinary laws; secondly, the global spread of constitutional review (currently adopted by 158 out of the 192 states members of the UN); and thirdly, the inclusion of ethical and normative principles in the dictate of the constitution: moral principles are legally recognized as statutory rules that public policies are called upon to enforce and promote. The formal conception of the constitution, according to which it is conceived as a way *to articulate, distinguish and limit the powers of the state*, is thus replaced by a substantial conception, according to which the main task of any constitution is *to recognize, enforce and preserve the fundamental rights of all citizens*.

As we will see in the present section, the evolution of this paradigm shift is similar to that considered in the case of liberalism – after all, both constitutionalism and liberalism maintain an essential link to the state as an institutional framework: the rise of modern states is essentially linked to their constitutional form, conceived as a legal structure that marks the borders and establishes the limits within which the political power may be legitimately exercised. In particular, criticism is levelled against the thesis of the neutrality of the law, according to which the law can be – and should be – described as a value-free dimension, that is, independently of any possible judgement of its content. The law can be neutral only in the sense that, by mirroring a given set of values that are actually shared by all the members of a given context, everyone can identify with the principles that represent the ethical core of the constitution. By rejecting the perspective according to which a law is valid (that is, recognized as law) only if approved by an institution specifically created and authorized to legislate, or at least if produced in accordance with certain formal procedures, constitutionalism conceives law as something that must meet and recognize a set of principles and values, which constitute the backbone of the political community that the law is called upon to translate into formal rules.

To say it otherwise, a given legal order cannot be valid just because it consists in a set of rules connected with each other and produced by the same source. In order to be valid – that is, to represent a consistent and legitimate form of social organization – a legal order must necessarily refer to substantive principles that may determine both the content of the norms and their application. It remains an open question whether the law, which has to recognize these principles and turn them into binding norms, must be considered an autonomous and self-sufficient system, or rather the legal recognition of a determinate form of life, whose ethical identity it has to reflect and safeguard.

After the subject and the object of politics (see, respectively, 1.1.1 and 1.1.2), then, we have now to focus on the changing face of the primary means of politics, i.e. the law. With regard to this, some authors state that the law constitutes a self-sufficient system. Others argue that an ethical and identitarian foundation of the norms represents a basic condition of possibility for any effective and comprehensive legal order. The opposition is thus between a formal conception of the constitution, according to which it is interpreted as the most effective way *to limit, control and restrain the government*, and a substantial conception, which sees in the constitution *the only means available to filter, orient and substantiate the political action*.

We can thus trace a continuum among different approaches to the relationship between legal order and normative principles. At one end of the spectrum we have what may be defined as a thin conception of the constitutional order (at one and the same time, systematic and formal), which goes back to the Enlightenment requirement for a clearly defined and rigidly structured legal order. At the other end, on the contrary, we have a substantive concept of the constitutional law (at once pragmatic and significant), according to which the primary aim of the highest law is to identify, single out and translate into legal norms the basic normative principles that lie at the heart of a given political community. Without being exhaustive and just to give an idea of the different perspectives, an example of the continuum in question may be the following (from classical constitutionalism to new constitutionalism): Luigi Ferrajoli (2007), Jürgen Habermas (1996, 1998), Carlos S. Nino (1996), Neil MacCormick (2007), Gustavo Zagrebelsky (1992), Robert Alexy (2002), Ronald Dworkin (1985, 1986), Ernst-Wolfgang Böckenförde (1991).

Although in a quite different way, all these theories try to answer the following basic question: once fundamental rights have been recognized as binding and superordinated legal norms, how is it possible to settle the major dispute between the law as it is and the law as it ought to be, that is, between *binding norms* and *programmatic norms* enforced within the same legal order? What is more, the inclusion of programmatic norms in the dictate of the constitution opens up a gap between formal and substantial validity. This gap in turn raises the question of how these norms should be interpreted: Are they *procedural rules for the passing of new laws* or rather *substantial prescriptions concerning the very content of the laws*? In other words, the question is how to create a link – which is now necessarily required within the very statutory law – between formal validity and substantial justice. As we will see below, two main solutions have been proposed: *the inclusion of principles of justice in the dictate of the constitution* and *the ethical interpretation of constitutional law*.

A discussion of all the approaches mentioned above goes beyond the limits of the present book. Our purpose is rather to sketch the general lines of the debate. To do so, we will briefly introduce the two most relevant and debated theories of the continuum: the concept of the democratic rule of law developed by Jürgen Habermas and the moral reading of the constitution proposed by Ronald Dworkin. Before dealing with these two theories, it is worth noting that the increasing relevance of, and the leading role assumed by constitutions in general and high courts in particular can be interpreted as the outcome of two main processes. First, it is due to the enforcement of a wider and wider spectrum of basic rights (charts, conventions, programmes), today not only recognized for individuals but also for well-defined social categories and political groups; secondly, the expansion of the judiciary sphere appears to be the most effective way to govern critical transitions and ensure normative stability by reducing the uncertainty and unpredictability of the decision-making process on a global scale, once the social, institutional and normative whole represented by the state – that is, the political mechanism to handle and settle conflicts of very different kind – has been shattered (Stone Sweet 2000).

The theory of law and democracy developed by Jürgen Habermas is meant to combine the original Kantian position with the demands of consequentialism and the inclusion of a (weakly) communitarian perspective. This approach is based on the *discourse ethics*, formulated by Habermas himself with the German philosopher Karl-Otto Apel. According to the Habermasian version of discourse ethics, what he terms 'ideal speech situation' is the only legitimate context for the argument, which is in turn a form of deliberation meant to reach the broadest possible consensus on what is true and what is right on the basis of rational procedures and in the absence of any form of coercive influence.

Habermas accounts for what he calls the *logical genesis of rights*, that is, the fact that the recognition of basic rights, conceived as inalienable prerogatives and freedoms which everyone as a communicative agent possesses, is logically implied by the combination of the *discourse principle* and the *medium of law*. The discourse principle, which is presented as a post-metaphysical reappraisal of the Kantian principle of universalizability, aims at accounting for the validity of norms: a norm is justified, and thus valid, only if all those affected by the foreseeable consequences of its adoption could accept it in a reasonable and public discourse. The medium of the law gives legitimacy to the political decision and provides it with its binding force using the threat of sanctions. By stabilizing forms of interaction that are based on generalized expectations of behaviour, the law makes any form of self-interested actions carried out by individuals explainable and predictable. The *democratic principle*, which is the normative outcome of the combination of the discourse principle and the medium of law, states that only those legal norms that can meet with the assent of all citizens in a discursive process of legislation that in turn has been legally constituted may claim legitimacy.

The democratic principle is meant to ensure that practical issues are fairly addressed and deliberated in a rational way. A process of ruling can be said to be discursively legitimate if and only if the following three features are present: being ideally unlimited in time and space (that is, open to all arguments and speakers); being able to grant and require equal rights and duties to all in the communicative interaction (that is, everyone has the right to speak and a duty to listen to the other speakers); and being conducted by cooperative peers who are willing to adopt plans of action that prove to be mutually compatible. A process of ruling, on the other hand, can be said to be legally structured if it provides both *sanctions against* strategic conduct and *reasons for* the adoption of an agreement-oriented behaviour.

In the Habermasian perspective, the tension between facticity and normativity is but the contraposition between the law as a binding command and the law as a legitimate rule: the mutual relationship between legal structure and the discourse principle is meant to fill the gap between these two different dimensions. According to Habermas, then, the state and the law are mutually complementary: on the one hand, the former ensures the enforcement of what has been decided, by using the threat of sanctions; on the other hand and at the same time, the latter provides the deliberation procedures and the legitimating conditions that the former needs.

Habermas argues that the only way to combine facts and norms is by interpreting them through the lens of a legal framework that he calls the *system of rights*. According to this peculiar approach, basic rights and legal procedures, far from being mutually exclusive, are in fact *co-original and complementing principles*. If this is true, private autonomy (fundamental rights) and public self-determination (popular sovereignty) imply one another, so that the one without the other can neither be conceived nor achieved or preserved. Accordingly, basic rights are no longer conceived as limits on the publicly justifiable exercise of democratic power, but rather as *conditions of possibility for the empowerment of autonomous subjects who recognize each other as co-responsible partners in dialogue*. To substantiate his view, Habermas deduces five categories of rights that are essential to any democratic rule of law: individual liberties, citizenship rights, due process rights, political rights and welfare rights (this latter category is justified, according to Habermas, only relatively and contingently, that is, exclusively in light of the need to secure the enjoyment of the remaining rights).

From an institutional standpoint, the democratic rule of law proposed by Habermas consists in a constitutional framework aimed at drawing the borders of the democratic field, that is, at distinguishing between what can be legitimately decided and what cannot. These borders are secured by basic rights conceived as conditions of possibility for the production and revision of norms. It follows that the only prerogatives, resources and conditions to be constitutionally recognized are those that prove to be necessary to create an informed and reflective public opinion and to ensure a constant revision (and ideally a never-ending improvement) of the rules of the game. What makes the democratic rule of law proposed by Habermas a critical and reflective theory is mainly this double function of the law, according to which the system of rights is intended as both the essential precondition and the ultimate outcome of the democratic discourse.

An alternative perspective to the *democratic rule of law* developed by Habermas is provided by the so-called *new constitutionalism*.

According to this different perspective, which challenges the primacy of the representative organs reaffirmed by Habermas, constitutions and constitutional courts are to be considered respectively *the firmest foundation* (and not only the source of the sources) and *the highest power* (and not merely the neutral power) on which contemporary liberal democracies rest. As a result, the constitution, as interpreted by the highest court, provides all the legal guidelines that are needed to regulate the social interactions on which a given communitarian context is based. The new constitutionalism directly challenges the traditional concepts of the validity, nature and interpretation of the law. Let us consider these transformations in more detail.

According to the advocates of new constitutionalism, the *validity of the law* is based on the necessary connection between statutory law on the one hand and the principles of justice and common good on the other. The normative or ethical content of the constitution is in turn substantiated and safeguarded by the enforcement of a given set of fundamental rights, the preservation of specific institutional practices and the adoption of consistent judicial interpretations. What makes a law the law is not primarily the formal deduction from a superior law, the reference to a legislative source or the compliance with predetermined procedures, but the substantial respect for a given set of principles and values, which constitute the ethical core of the communitarian context and a *substantial precondition for the realization and stabilization of a well-ordered society.*

New constitutionalists are divided on which is the ultimate source of the principles of justice. According to the new constitutionalists who make reference to the natural law jurisprudence, these principles are immanent in nature and their validity is logically prior to and normatively independent of their recognition by an enforced legal order. According to the new constitutionalists who adhere to legal positivism, on the contrary, there are principles of justice if and only if a legal order turns them in a consistent set of norms and, by that very fact, recognizes their existence, validity and binding character.

Accordingly, the *nature of the law* cannot be reduced to a set of simple precepts. On the contrary, it must be extended to the justification of what is dictated: it has to provide for *cogent and plausible reasons to act as the rule prescribes*. This is required by the endorsement of a different concept of law, according to which, as we have seen above, formal validity is complemented (and, to some degree, replaced) by substantial validity, which tends to reflect and perpetuate, as a sort of normative synthesis, the main ethical features characterizing a given community. Because of (what is considered to be) its self-evidence, it is reasonable to expect that the crucial importance and the substantial justice of this ethical-legal basis can be not only properly assessed by judges but also easily understood by lay citizens.

Finally, the *interpretation of the law* consists primarily in a legal balancing of fundamental rights that may be conflicting at the moment but that, in the long run, are equally required for the achievement of a well-ordered society, since they represent the ethical core of the whole community. By rejecting one of the basic theoretical pillars of legal positivism, judicial interpretation, as conceived by new constitutionalism, excludes any form of judicial discretion: there exists always the possibility of a right answer (*the* right answer), or at least of an adequate answer inspired by the letter and the spirit of the constitution. What is more, this answer cannot be deduced by inference from a superior norm, but is to be found in the way social interactions are shaped and conducted.

Essentially, this innovative way to conceive the role of the constitution within a wider political context is based on two main tenets: the *over-interpretation of the constitution* and the *constitutionalization of the legal order*. According to the first tenet, judicially affirmed rights are not only legal guarantees, but first and foremost a major source for political action and a great force of social change. What is more, there is no moral or political conflict that cannot be translated into legal terms and solved in judicial contexts. As Aharon Barak – the president of the Israeli Supreme Court from 1995 to 2006 – paradigmatically stated, 'Nothing falls beyond the purview of judicial review. The world is filled with law; everything and anything is justiciable'. The second tenet refers to the fact that the normative guidelines and values contained in the constitution (whether implicitly or explicitly) actually and rightfully determine the action of the government (by shaping public policies), the activities of the parliament (by urging the adoption of specific measures) and the role of the jurisprudence (by interpreting the law) within a given political context.

The constitution is thus no longer conceived as the ultimate and not-open-to-appeal way to determine and fix the prerogatives, roles and limits of the powers of the state, but rather as the guardian of the ethical principles on which the political community is grounded. This reassessment of the essence and value of the constitution has a very important consequence. If the constitution is now conceived as a sort of hermeneutical tool and normative device that, by recognizing and including the different interests of the various parties involved, proves to be able to effectively manage social conflicts among groups, it is (or at least can be) no longer dependent, in the last resort, on the enforcement of a state legal order. This conception of the constitutional jurisprudence, by opening up to the possibility of a global legal order based on the recognition and enforcement of a cross-cultural set of fundamental rights, marks the end of the essential and exclusive link between the law and the state and opens up to new forms of regulation, essentially intended to inscribe new 'constitutional' actors (mostly corporate power and financial agents) in the legal world order (Gill and Cutler 2014).

An influential version of new constitutionalism can be found in the writings of Ronald Dworkin, according to which the law is neither a system of rules nor a sum of legal adjudications, but a complex social practice that is based on principles and values shared by the different actors involved in the practice itself. By adopting a hermeneutic approach (that is the view that legal practice is in its nature interpretive), Dworkin argues that the interpreter has to take into account what the participants in the practice take it to mean, although the concept of law cannot be reduced to the conventional understanding of a given interaction. Within this perspective, the best interpretation is that which is sensitive both to the facts of the practices and to the values or principles that the practices serve and in the light of which the individual behaviour can be consistently explained.

According to the *moral reading of the constitution* he proposes, the constitution is to be conceived as a set of rights provisions that refer to abstract moral principles, the interpretation of which must ultimately appeal to the moral or political theory that proves to be most consistent with the text or practice at stake. This immanent link between constitutional norms and communitarian practices is what permits the *reflexivity of both the legal process and the social context in which it takes place*. The constitutional judge is thus called upon to give the best interpretation of the ethical principles to which the constitution more or less explicitly refers. Such an interpretation must consistently combine the moral practices and the constitutional tradition that characterize a given communitarian context with the demands of justice implied by the legal case under investigation, without thereby violating those principles of justice that represent the distinctive features of the community (as they are expressed by the constitutional texts, the self-understanding of the legal practice, the previous legal cases and the actual history of the community itself).

But what about the risk of an overwhelming power in the judiciary? To overcome this possible objection, Dworkin argues that legal reasoning and legal interpretation are in their essence deliberative, that is, open to deliberation, criticism and discussion. If it is true that, according to Dworkin's *right answer thesis*, a correct approach to legal questions allows a necessary answer for each individual, this means neither that there will be just one correct answer nor that the same answer will be justified and defended in the same way by all its advocates. The constitutional text provides relevant principles, not clear-cut indications. This gap makes room for challenge and criticism: legal scholars and interpreters can reject a legal interpretation that seems to them at odds (or less consistent than others) with the history and traditions of their community.

The constitutional judges, then, are called upon to achieve an equitable balance between, on the one hand, the spirit of the constitution and the communitarian traditions and, on the other hand, the different sensibilities of their fellow citizens about the meaning and relevance of the concrete case under dispute. By complying with the constitution, the judges safeguard the core values and principles of the political community. At the same time, by being attentive to what the other members of the community think, feel and demand, they prevent the risk that the constitution may become an absolute constraint on legislators and the present legal order a mere reproduction of the constituent will. Thanks to this reasonable and fair balance between conservation and innovation, the overall consistency and integrity of the law are preserved. Far from being a hermeneutic approach to past practices, legal interpretation opens up to the future: any legal decision is called upon to combine and harmonize the long-established communitarian traditions with the demands of new public policies.

Finally, within the hermeneutic perspective developed by Dworkin, the conflict between legal validity and normative legitimacy seems to disappear. Indeed, it is true that Dworkin famously states that rights are trumps and as such they must prevail whenever any right comes into conflict with any policy or functional requirement, including the democratic procedures for deliberation. Yet, the need for constitutional review that follows (legal validity) is presented by Dworkin more as a means to reaffirm superior principles of justice and even as an integral part of these very principles (normative legitimacy) than as an external and conflicting requirement of justice. Within this perspective, constitutionalism and democracy, far from representing two potentially conflicting domains, share a basic principle and contribute in different ways and with different means to its promotion. According to this principle, on which any public policy should be based, every person is entitled to an equal status as a citizen. This means that both the judiciary and representative organs must treat citizens with *equal concern and respect*. As a result, the rejection of an unjust law should be intended as the primary aim of any legitimate government. Again, constitutional judges are called upon to go beyond the contingent preferences of their fellow citizens and to adopt a forward-looking and more systematic perspective, aimed at safeguarding and preserving those principles of justice on which the political community is based and which secure also the freedom of the dissenting members. This difference in framing and managing public decisions is what makes the judicial interpretation not merely legitimate but also the most reliable solution.

In our opinion, it is evident that new constitutionalism, conceived as a legal practice aimed at establishing a legal framework based on just laws and a fair adjudication of conflicting demands, is grounded on two ill-concealed and highly disputable claims. 1) Everyone, as both a rational agent and a member of the community, is expected to share the substantive and actually self-evident outcome achieved by the democratic procedures adopted in a well-ordered society. 2) Especially if compared to the political power and role of the parliament, the judicial power and the constitution of a liberal democracy – as grounded on a limited and consistent set of basic rights and moral values – prove to be the most effective, reliable and impartial system for safeguarding and promoting this outcome and, in particular, for settling disputes concerning fundamental moral questions, contested public policies and long-lasting political controversies.

From a critical point of view, these assumptions create serious problems, with regard to both internal consistency and normative legitimacy.

As to the internal consistency, the problem is that the principles of justice under dispute cannot be considered as legal rules since they are not (necessarily) included in the dictate of the constitution. As a consequence, among other things, they are not hierarchically ordered. The non-legal (or at least quasi-legal) character of these principles necessarily makes room for an ambiguous recognition of the 'normative force of facts' and for some highly discretionary forms of ethical intuitionism, which are adopted by judicial organs to settle disputes concerning the most appropriate balance among different ethical principles. Equally unclear is how a possible conflict between conflicting interpretations about the true ethical and political identity of a communitarian context can be solved, once every formal and value-free procedure of deliberation has been dismissed.

As to the normative legitimacy, from a democratic standpoint, this near-sacred status attributed to the constitution does not lead to a strict observance of the dictate of the law, but rather to the weakening of the very constitution whose legal force is reduced to a set of ethical guidelines. The focus on this motley array of programming statements ends up seriously undermining the guaranteeing function of the constitution and the democratic system as a whole. As a consequence, an unrestrained judicial power becomes a sort of *court of last resort in all questions of ethical relevance*. Courts are assigned the demiurgic power of redefining the prerogatives of, and redrawing the boundaries between, the different state powers without being subjected to the scrutiny of any democratic oversight mechanism. As a result, the judiciary system turns out to be, at one and the same time, one of the branches provided by the constitution and the organ that has the power of actually reshaping the constitutional distinction and separation between representative, executive and judiciary prerogatives.

1.2 Justice and injustices

1.2.1 New paradigms of justice

The fundamental evolutions we have considered thus far lead to a further major change. A relevant set of political prerogatives, functions and tasks traditionally carried out by the state are now transferred and assigned to other social spheres and agencies. The essential aim of this transfer, at least from a public point of view, is to implement basic social policies, once pursued within the different national contexts, beyond national borders, in order to counter, at least in part, the decline of the state. This is particularly the case of certain questions and demands of justice, which remain unsatisfied at a state level and are thus framed and addressed in the supranational context. The question is then how to secure conditions of justice and non-domination once the material, organizational and normative resources of the state appear to be more and more limited.

Supported by the increasing (and far from unproblematic) attention paid in the past decades to the necessity of safeguarding fundamental rights at the international level, the attempt to enforce principles of justice on a global scale has led to the development of two new comprehensive paradigms of justice: *global justice* (here limited to international distributive justice), which conceives of fundamental rights as *regulative principles of international politics*; and *transitional justice*, which conceives of fundamental rights as *justiciable provisions*. These perspectives share a *restorative* conception of justice, according to which the fundamental task of justice is to re-establish mutual responsibility and confidence for constructive responses to wrongdoing that may preserve the safety and dignity of all. The common aim is thus to demonstrate, on the one hand, the injustice, irrationality and ineffectiveness of the redistributive and administrative policies traditionally adopted and, on the other hand, the necessity to move from the current *redistributive paradigms based on allocation* to *redistributive programmes based on compensation*.

The emergence of the question of a supranational justice, in the two forms we are going to consider, is mainly a consequence of the major changes that occurred in the world order and in the way policies of social justice were justified and defended (from a normative standpoint) after the fall of communism and the spread of globalization.

As to normative legitimacy, the liberal and the socialist democratic policies implemented by the state involved a manifest contradiction. On the one hand, they based their legitimacy on the moral equality of all individuals as inherent to all human beings, independently of any other condition or feature. On the other hand, and at the same time, the states granted and limited this recognition, along with the legal guarantees and the social services it entailed, only to their citizens, within a well-defined and restricted space. National membership, conceived as a special relationship between a person and their place of birth, was thus completely at odds with the concept of the equality of the human person developed and defended by both liberals and democrats. What is more, it appeared to be as morally indifferent as the race, the gender and the social class – that is to say, if compared to those criteria of discrimination that the rule of law had outlawed after a long struggle.

When the models of government and the public policies adopted by the states in the last century fall into crisis, the contradiction between a universalist conception of the fundamental rights and their limited application leads to the recognition of the fact that questions of justice (along with our moral duties) go beyond national borders. Their *primary* focus is (or at least should be) on the relations among human beings and not on those among citizens. The increasing awareness that the resources of the earth are sufficient to meet the needs of all humankind but are provided and exploited in a highly unequal manner becomes the cornerstone of most global theories. Its normative translation can be found in the general principle according to which each individual ought to have an equal amount of natural resources.

As to the changing face of the world order at the end of the last century, four major transformations must be mentioned: the spread of liberal democracy throughout the world after the fall of communism; the related hegemony of the capitalist system on the global scale; the accelerated compression of space and time in the globalized world; and the increasing mobility and transnational migration of people and capital. These processes have led to a strict interdependence of the different levels of interactions (national, transnational and supranational). As a result, questions concerning the regulation of financial and labour markets, the legislation on property rights and international trade, monetary policies, rules on the use of armed force and on the distribution of natural resources – all these become systemic needs which can no longer be regulated exclusively at the national level (that is, through inter-state agreements or multilateral treaties).

As soon as the forms of supranational governance characterizing the traditional inter-state system prove unable to manage the new global processes (see 2.2.1), the different global actors realize that the consequences of political decisions, legal responsibilities, military threats and social inequalities have relevant impacts well beyond the original context. This must be understood as a two-way relationship: internal affairs have far-reaching and long-term consequences at the global level and the other way around.

Given the plurality of views and approaches about what is normatively relevant or valuable in the supranational domain, not only do theories of global justice differ in kind, but there are important differences among individual theories of a given kind. The debate substantially reflects the differences that exist between the various theories of distributive justice at a national level. Accordingly, while all the theories of global justice aim at establishing a more egalitarian system of distribution and sharing of natural and economic resources (although differently shaped), they differ on what is to be granted to whom and by whom. Let us briefly consider these issues in more detail.

What is to be granted? Overall, the choice is between *primary resources and goods* (in a Rawlsian sense) – that is, basic goods that meet the fundamental needs of individuals (*rights to resources*), in their turn divided into material resources and interpersonal relationships that are considered as essential bases of self-respect – and *rights of political participation and social inclusion* that follow from membership in cooperative networks (*relational rights*) and are assumed to be necessary conditions to reach a consensus about what counts as a primary good.

Who is entitled to get what must be granted? According to *supranational institutionalism* (Nagel 2005), the basic goods must be granted only to people that mutually participate in shared institutions and relate to each other within the same interactional context (that may be coextensive with the state itself). According to this perspective, a shared cultural framework (and mostly common traditions and a common coercive legal system) is an essential condition to get the amount of resources, organizational effort and social cohesion (in terms of legitimacy and solidarity) that is actually necessary to ensure an equitable and fair distribution. This form of institutionalism is challenged by the advocates of a *global egalitarianism* (Caney 2005), according to which what is relevant is only the moral status of individuals as human agents, independent of the different relationships they may have at different levels with other individuals.

Accordingly, in the institutionalist perspective, the community of legitimate recipients of distributive policies is defined as comprising exclusively the members of a limited and well-defined interactional context, while within the egalitarian perspective cultural, legal and political borders play no role at all (an interesting attempt to mediate between these two positions is represented by the *pluralist internationalism* advanced in Risse 2012).

Finally, who should be the provider, that is, who has both the duty and the right to perform the distribution? According to the *internationalist theories*, the principles of justice to be enforced beyond the borders of the national communities must be debated and established within the deliberative context of the state, in order to ensure, through a polycentric system of distribution, the basic conditions for cultural and legal pluralism (Miller 2007). In contrast to the internationalist approach, the *globalist theories* argue that the principles of justice should not only be applied but also established beyond the state (Pogge 2008). This version of distributive globalism may in turn be divided into radical globalism and weak globalism. Radical globalism recognizes an immediate relationship between global institutions and individuals (or, to say it in another way, the communitarian context is described as coextensive with the earth) and calls for the establishment of democratic global institutions that may replace the existing states and allow world citizens to participate more directly in political life. Weak globalism, on the other hand, recognizes only a mediate relationship between a limited set of supranational institutions and individuals, and calls for a more or less radical reform of both the existing supranational agencies and the patterns of interaction between them and the states.

In what follows, some key aspects of the global justice will be further discussed in a brief presentation of Thomas Pogge's view on the global poverty (2008, 2010). What is particularly interesting, to our purposes, is the direct relationship that exists between the development programmes and multilateral effort led (mostly) by Western states to aid developing countries (in this case to eradicate poverty) – and more generally, the patterns of interaction that connect the two contexts – and the perpetuation and reinforcement of the existing asymmetry of power between the two fronts. In particular, Pogge emphasizes how these particular inter-state relations decisively contribute, on the one hand, to establishing a political order internal to the developing countries that may serve the worldwide interests of Western elites and, on the other hand, to perpetuate these very elites as leading and privileged agents in the political life of the developed countries and, more generally, in the global arena. In short, Pogge's analysis allows us to consider how the emergence of subnational groups decisively alters the relations of power at a supranational level and the other way round.

The argument developed by Pogge – whose cosmopolitanism can be considered as a moral theory targeted at institutions (see 2.2.1) – is based on three main tenets. 1) The local social factors – endemic corruption, financial mismanagement, bad government – which are usually considered to be a decisive contributory cause of the persistence of severe poverty in the less-developed countries, do not represent wholly endogenous ingredients of a lesser culture, but are *structurally* facilitated and even sustained by core features of the present global order, created and imposed by a small circle of financial and political elites through some key international institutions (above all, the WTO). 2) Resources and borrowing privileges – through which autocrats and local militias can alienate natural resources and get access to international credit in the name of the country and its people – are granted by the international community to anyone who happens to rise to power in the less-developed countries (independently of any standard of legitimacy and accountability), in order to serve the interests of both local authorities and Western countries at the expense of the local population's well-being and rights. 3) The less developed countries need help only because of the gross injustices the most developed countries have been inflicting upon them.

To turn to the basic issue of the present chapter – the question of justice – Pogge contends that the real injustice consists in the imposition on poor people (who are thus unable to oppose and challenge this attempt) of a structurally coercive and unfair global order, decided by Western governments and in the name of the peoples they represent. The World Bank estimated that in 2008 1.29 billion people lived conditions of extreme poverty (while poverty decreases, social and economic inequality increases in all areas of the world). According to Pogge, since Western countries actively shape and enforce the social conditions that foreseeably and avoidably cause the suffering of a large part of the world, they are *intentionally harming* the people who live in developing countries. As active participants, Western countries are not simply disregarding their positive duties to help, but are actually violating their negative duties not to harm. Pogge concludes that the imposition of the present global order represents the largest crime against humanity ever committed. Accordingly, corrective measures must not be conceived as forms of assistance, but as consistent procedures to protect the poor from the exploitative forces that are at the service of the existing international institutions.

Within this perspective, then, the policies carried out by the developed nations at a global level are *directly* responsible for the condition of disadvantage and discrimination of the underdeveloped countries. Again, Pogge emphasizes that Western countries must be called to account for what they have done (*outcome responsibility*) – that is, for the exploitative system they have struggled to establish on a global scale – and not simply for what they have been unable to prevent (*remedial responsibility*) – that is, for the failed attempts to save millions of people from starvation. To say it otherwise, the present well-being of the developed nations essentially depends on the perpetuation of the existing asymmetry of power and resources between them and the rest of the world, from which it follows that a radical reform of the existing global order turns out to be an essential precondition for eliminating, or at least reducing, world poverty.

Pogge suggests two specific corrective measures, which must be considered as preliminary and temporary measures to be implemented for regulating the existing asymmetries of power until a structural and definitive reform of the whole global order can be achieved.

The first measure to tackle world poverty is the implementation of a *global resources dividend*. According to this proposal, states would remain the legal owners of the natural resources present in their territories but, as a form of compensation to be granted to the most disadvantaged nations, they would pay a dividend on the amount of resources they use, sell or simply waste. Pogge conceives this measure of compensation as the natural translation on a global scale of the difference principle which Rawls, by denying both the legitimacy and the opportunity of such a normative extension, has restricted to national contexts. According to Rawls, states have no redistributive duties at all but merely a duty of assistance, which he never accepts as a truly binding political obligation (Rawls 1999).

The second measure proposed by Pogge is the reform of the current normative regime on intellectual property rights (TRIPS) as an opportunity to completely reshape the pharmaceutical patent system. The underlying normative assumption is that health research should be considered a global common good and, as such, shared for free and for the benefit of all people. To provide a market-based solution to the existing patent system, Pogge proposes a health impact fund, financed by the most-developed countries, meant to incentivize and reward, according to their measurable contribution to reduce the global burden of disease, the (otherwise economically counterproductive) research and development of new pharmaceutical products by market-oriented corporations.

The other fundamental pillar of the new paradigms of justice based on the essential link between state level and global level is *transitional (or reconstructive) justice.* The discussion of this much-debated approach to justice allows us to shed further light on the evolution of contemporary political practices and their relationship with the law and the newly emerging forms of social integration. This peculiar paradigm of justice consists in judicial and non-judicial practices, procedures and decisions (criminal prosecutions, truth commissions, compensations for damages, reparation programmes, recovery plans, political and social reforms) that are adopted to punish those responsible for gross human-rights violations and redress victims of psychological and physical abuses perpetrated, in most cases, by authoritarian regimes (Teitel 2002) or occupying forces (Roht-Arriaza and Mariezcurrena 2006). Why transitional and reconstructive? This kind of justice can be termed 'transitional' because the measures in question are usually implemented at the moment of a political transition from a previous authoritarian regime to a newly established democratic (or at least less authoritarian) political system. The term 'reconstructive', instead, refers to the fundamental aim of rebuilding mutual trust and restoring social cohesion among individuals.

Transitional justice is comprised of two branches, pursuing two different aims. While *criminal processes* aim at removing from power and punishing those responsible for the most serious crimes, *civil processes* aim at finding various forms of compensation for the damage caused to the victims of the criminal behaviour. Damage may be material (loss of goods), personal (violation of personal integrity and freedom) or intangible (loss of opportunities and capabilities).

A brief discussion of the development of transitional justice will allow us to focus on the radical and far-reaching consequences this process has had in the way the political sphere has been framed and conceived in recent years, with particular regard to its boundaries, tasks and functions.

Transitional justice takes upon itself a task of titanic proportions: it aims at taking History to the Court and prosecuting not only its main protagonists but even entire political systems and historical periods. Within this perspective, history is no longer the court of judgement of the world, as Hegel famously claimed, but, quite on the contrary, what must be assessed through legal adjudications. The advocates of transitional justice claim that no ongoing injustice or perpetrated abuse falls outside of the legal domain and its forms of persecution. Accordingly, even history and its symbolic legacy become a judicial matter. Within the perspective in question, the law in its different articulations is claimed to be able to restore, at least potentially, any form and condition of justice. The most serious risk inherent in this approach is the *judicialization of politics*, an issue to which we will return.

After the epochal processes of Nuremberg (1945–6) and Tokyo (1946–8), the contraposition between the USA and the USSR marks the end of similar trials. With the end of the Cold War, the prospect of a supranational court again comes to the fore. As a result, two ad hoc courts have recently been established to prosecute war crimes in two different contexts: the International Criminal Tribunal for the former Yugoslavia (ICTY) in 1993 and the International Criminal Tribunal for Rwanda (ICTR) in 1994. But this legal practice has gone a step further, marking a major turning point in international relations since the end of World War I. In the midst of the NATO bombing of Yugoslavia in 1999, and for the first time in history, a head of state *while still in office*, the President of the Federal Republic of Yugoslavia, Slobodan Milošević, was charged with crimes against humanity by an international court. From that moment on, international justice has no longer been conceived as a remedial practice, but first and foremost as a way to establish (and challenge) the legitimacy of existing political regimes. Shortly thereafter, on 1 July 2002, the permanent tribunal of International Criminal Court (ICC) came into force. Finally, during the Libyan civil war in 2011, the same Court issued an international arrest warrant for Muammar Gaddafi.

From an ideal-typical point of view, transitional justice may impinge on a pure *political* justice or a pure *legal* justice (Elster 2004). The former is where the government of the new political course (or the occupying forces) designates the wrongdoers and decides what must be done with them or where the judges are called upon to determine the degree of guilt but not the existence of it (which is established in advance). By contrast, a pure legal justice is where: the laws are unambiguous (that is, the freedom of judges to decide what the law implies is much more limited than the freedom of legislators to decide what the law will be); the judiciary is really independent of the other powers; the laws are applied in an impartial and unbiased way; and the legal practices adhere strictly to the principles of due process.

As a matter of fact, it is very difficult adequately to determine the three essential requirements for the criminal process: the legal condition (the law that has been violated), the material condition (the crime that has been committed) and the psychological condition (the intention to do harm). But, even apart from these relevant aspects, the legal character of the processes under review is undermined by procedural and structural factors.

As far as the procedural factors are concerned, criminal trials as a retributive response to the wrongdoings committed by the government or the executives of a previous regime face the serious challenge of making retribution compatible with the basic principles of the rule of law. This is far from being an easy task. The creation of the International Criminal Court in 2002 has undoubtedly marked a historical milestone in the transnational effort to prosecute war

crimes. Yet, among other countries, the United States, Russia, China
and India do not intend to become state parties: they represent
more than half the world's population, the absolute majority in
the UN Security Council and almost 40 per cent of the world's
GDP. Furthermore, if the ratification of a long series of international treatises concerning the recognition of various fundamental
rights since the Universal Declaration of Human Rights in 1948 has
decisively contributed to countering the serious criticism that there
can be no crime committed without the previous violation of a legal
proscription that must have been in force when the alleged crime
was committed, considerable doubts remain about the legality of
this kind of criminal trial. The impossibility of an appeal against the
decision of the court, the role of the government in the selection of
both the judges and the accused, and the primacy of narrative and
testimonial knowledge over procedural debates and legal argumenta-
tions, are some of the problems associated with adopting criminal
processes to restore legality in times of crisis. By emphasizing these
essential features, some scholars have raised serious doubts about the
legitimacy of any attempt to translate criminal justice at a supranational level (Zolo 2009).

By contrast, the structural flaws are not due to an alleged lack
of legality but, more decisively, to an inevitable degree of ineffectiveness. Why inevitable? Essentially because more often than not
the processes in question are expected to achieve what are in fact
incompatible aims. Indeed, within the retributive perspective, trials
must be at one and the same time speedy, swift, severe, just, thorough,
efficacious, equitable and comprehensive. The problem is that many
of these requirements may come into conflict with one another and
also with other external and contextual constraints that further
limit their effectiveness in restoring social cohesion (Elster 2004).
To give a common example, the transition to a new political system
may require a certain degree of clemency by the court. As a result,

transitional justice, mostly in the case of criminal processes, is heavily constrained by essential trade-offs at both a normative and an extra-normative level. In particular, the hard lesson is that truth, peace and justice are at once the watchwords of an ambitious project of moral, social and political reconstruction and also, and more problematically, three conflicting imperatives (Bass 2002).

Whatever the judgement on the normative consistency and political convenience of such legal actions (Garapon 2002), it is a fact that the intertwining of the moral, political and legal aspects that characterize transitional justice marks the end of the Westphalian model of sovereignty. This new way of conceiving the international legal order and the strict relationship between the national and the supranational spheres gets rid of the three basic pillars of modern politics: the balance of power among different and equal political subjects, the rigid separation between moral and political domains, and the clear-cut distinction of internal and foreign affairs (modern international law deals only with disputes between states per se, in which the damaged party has the right to retaliate against the counterpart and, in case of victory, the right to claim reparations for war damages).

As a result – and this is a capital point – memory is no longer conceived as an essential precondition for justice, but as the essential aim of the legal action as a whole. This overturn leads to a performative paradox, according to which a legal discharge may be read as a way to deny recognition to the victims or to give legitimacy to the regime on trial.

The other and more recent branch of transitional justice deals with the different claims for compensation in civil actions brought by the victims and/or survivors of a criminal political conduct. Accordingly, the legal focus shifts from the wrongdoers to the victims. In 1996 a number of major Jewish associations in the United States filed a series of class actions against some Swiss banks,

German companies and other financial and industrial institutions that were accused of retaining and concealing assets looted from Holocaust victims. The total amount of compensation awarded was approximately eight billion dollars. More recently, similar legal actions have been announced against the states responsible for the transatlantic slave trade and the extermination campaigns conducted during the age of modern colonialism. In contrast to the former kind of claim, the advocates of this latter type argue that there is a causal link between the exploitation of their ancestors and their current condition as marginalized and actually excluded people. Moreover, the existential damage suffered by the heirs is claimed to be a lasting and permanent one. A first consequence of such actions is that while the death of the accused has the immediate effect of terminating the legal action, the death of the victims does not determine the same result. Civil process, as conceived in the perspective of transitional justice, allows anyone to appeal to any court in any moment (even in time of political stability) for any existential damage suffered in the past.

The focus of the legal action, then, shifts from wrongdoers to victims. The object is no longer the intention of the wrongdoer, but the damage suffered by the victim. Similarly, the subject is not the person accused but the goods she possesses. Finally the aim is not to punish the wrongdoers, but to compensate the victims. There are four main forms of reparation: restitution, compensation, rehabilitation and reassurance (Kritz 1995). *Restitution* aims to restore the status quo ante as far as individual rights, social status and personal properties are concerned. *Compensation* – undoubtedly the most widespread form – aims at compensating the actual damages resulting from the criminal conduct that are economically quantifiable. *Rehabilitation* consists in a series of public and non-public measures and services provided to aid victims both materially and psychologically. *Reassurance* consists in a series of public and non-public initiatives and policies for the prevention of possible future damaging acts.

Within this perspective, civil transitional justice appears to be based on the centuries-old liberal utopia – now dislocated in the legal field, after the rejection of a universally binding 'view from nowhere' internal to the public sphere – according to which any conflict can be procedurally and normatively reduced (or at least converted) to a simple conflict of private interests, which can in turn be translated into economic terms and settled with a cost–benefit perspective. As a result, political conflicts tend to become private disputes and guilt becomes a basic legal category to be replaced by the concept of economic debit as a new form of political neutrality (Garapon 2008).

In a similar way, public law tends to be replaced by a non-political and self-sufficient civil law, while political conflicts are likely to be overcome by a new public management based on a mix of legal technique and economic rationality. According to this radical programme, justice is but a relation, a given balance, between damage and the compensation for it, based on the possibility of turning anything into a payable credit. At the end of the day, then, transitional justice turns into an ambiguous form of transactional justice. This conversion opens the door to a new legal space, in which the norms are no longer the logical consequence of the enforced legal order, but the essential preconditions for the rise and development of a new transnational and reticular legal order.

Yet, the attempt to solve major political conflicts by legal means is seriously undermined by a basic contradiction. In fact, this innovative form of liberal neutrality pursues two incompatible aims. On the one hand, it intends to emphasize as much as possible the moral and political relevance of a given historical event or process; on the other hand and at the same time, it aims at neutralizing the disruptive and dramatic effects that an extra-legal reaction to such events may produce. In the deeply ambivalent attitude towards the state, adopted by this peculiar approach to justice, we can find the institutional consequence of this basic contradiction. Again, on the one hand, the state dimension is (said to be) overcome, and on the other hand, the very possibility of these legal actions essentially depends on peaceful conditions and stable institutions that only the state as a local agency can actually provide.

As hinted above, transitional justice is the most striking example of what has been called the *judicialization of politics* (Hirschl 2004). Essentially, it consists in a transfer of decision-making power from representative institutions to judiciaries at both a national and supra-national level. As a matter of fact, national tribunals and supranational courts are more and more becoming the ultimate and not-open-to-appeal political decision makers with regard to key questions of public policy, with main but not exclusive reference to fundamental rights (principles of due process, privacy guarantees, religious liberties and so on). This is particularly evident in the case of the specific set of issues and decisions that Hirschl (2008) has labelled 'mega-politics', that is, legal resolutions that decisively contribute to shaping the political course of a given community (for example by establishing or denying the legitimacy of a new institutional order).

The aim of a *de-politicization of political relations* is based on the judicial debate as the essential deliberative practice to establish what the main social issues are and how they must be assessed. Yet, there is a growing amount of evidence that such an overwhelming task cannot be performed without undermining both the legitimacy and the effectiveness of the whole legal system. For example, as far as transitional justice is concerned, a process that is required at the same time to give recognition to the victims, to honour the memory, to judge history and to rebuild a communitarian context, cannot accomplish these tasks without eroding the legal guarantees required by its role as a third party and facilitator between different and conflicting social subjects.

If this is true, the overlapping of legal and political functions, procedures and expertise turns out to be very dangerous. The judicialization of politics entails necessarily a *politicization of justice* (Ferejohn 2002), that is, a displacement of the political from its proper institutional location to a social domain (the legal field) completely unequipped to deal with it. To give one example, once negationism is made legally punishable, the courts are required to establish which are the true, correct and legitimate historical reconstructions. Although such legislation remains controversial, in some countries the denial of any act regarded by an international criminal court as genocide is punished with prison. Again, the difference between historical truth and legal truth seems to disappear.

Yet, the translation of essentially political tasks in legal terms (and their achievement by means of legal measures) fundamentally alters both the concept of justice and the space of politics. In other words, far from being a neutral tool that can be used in quite different contexts and for very different aims, the law inevitably transforms the social reality it is called upon to manage and order. This sort of compulsory administration of the political sphere by the legal field does not lead to a de-politicization of conflicts (let alone to a greater degree of cohesion between conflicting parts), but to a precarious situation in which social stability is at risk and the necessary and mutual balance between the two domains is seriously undermined. In our opinion, such a failure proves once again the absolute necessity of politics as a way to envisage debate and agree on effective solutions. Of course, this represents not only a guarantee but also a problem. Yet, any adequate answer to social conflicts necessarily requires the mediation of politics, which is called upon to take charge, transform and meet different social demands and needs.

Finally, the vantage point of transitional justice allows us to take a fresh look at two of the most innovative and debated issues of contemporary political philosophy: the ethical and cognitive

function of *emotions* in the political sphere and the social role played
by the *recognition* of the different but shared dimensions of (what is
considered to be) human identity.

As far as emotions are concerned, a growing body of text has been
emphasizing the interdependence between emotions and cognition,
as well as their political relevance in the public debate. According to
these authors, normative as well as analytical approaches to politics
should take into due consideration the crucial role of narrative
imagination in ethical, political and legal questions. Indeed, only
through narrative accounts – conceived as a way to represent and
communicate one's own experiences and values without losing their
true meaning – are the political subjects able to configure and
share their personal and very different conceptions of the good life.
Within this perspective, politics deals primarily with emotions and
feelings and not with rational arguments or basic goods. Accordingly,
political theory must open up to narrative texts and other forms of
artistic representations (Nussbaum 2001).

As far as the role played by recognition is conceived, it may be
described as an alternative way to redress psychological or physical
abuses. Within this perspective, the injustice is not conceived
primarily as loss of some good, but rather as misrecognition of
one's personhood and humanity. Accordingly, restoration of justice
does not mean (primarily) redistribution of basic goods, but recognition of personal agency. This aim can be achieved by shaping
and enforcing the social conditions that prove to be necessary for
individuals to understand themselves as human agents, that is, as free
and equal subjects who interact with other free and equal subjects.
The focus shifts from individual civil and political liberties as simple
(and, of course, fundamental) legal guarantees to personal autonomy
and self-esteem as the ultimate outcome of a more complex and
far-reaching process of mutual recognition among interdependent
social actors (Fraser and Honneth 2003; Honneth 1995).

1.2.2 Sovereignty in transition

But if justice – considered by many as the political goal *par excellence* – has become a central concern of the supranational domain and if it is actually debated and addressed at the international level, what is left of the state? How does it serve, if ever, its political functions? In this section, we will try to answer this basic question by focusing on the two main prerogatives of modern sovereignty: the *recognition of citizenship* (domestic authority) and the *resort to war* (external authority). As we will see, these prerogatives have been undergoing a deep reassessment owing to the emergence of new social groups, both internal and external to the state, with different needs and demands.

The question of citizenship has again come to the fore in recent years in response to two main processes. The first is the growth of immigrant communities internal to the social context of the country of destination as an effect of the reunification of family members of the growing number of foreign or migrant workers. The second is the increasing number of identitarian claims and social demands mainly advanced by indigenous communities and refugees. These changes have proved the need to develop a new concept of citizen and to combine new forms of citizenship with multilevel migration and integration policies, openly challenged by the unexpected resurgence of nationalism in very different contexts (Bauböck 1994; Soysal 1994).

The modern concept of citizenship – grounded in the exclusive and indissoluble relation between each individual and the state – is thus challenged by very different social movements. These groups, in the name of specific interests and/or inherent identities, claim citizenship rights *not in spite of, but precisely because of their cultural difference*. The policies of *assimilation*, based on a one-way relationship between receiving countries and migrants, are more and more being replaced by comprehensive policies of *integration*. The latter are based on a two-way relationship, according to which the interaction between the different institutions of the receiving countries and the education of migrants brings far-reaching changes in the way the institutional framework is modelled and personal identities are conceived. As a result, new models and concepts of citizenship have been emerging in recent years. For our purposes, the most interesting are the concepts of denationalized citizenship and postnational citizenship.

Denationalized citizenship is an umbrella term for different new citizenship processes which challenge the exclusive relationship between the individual as a citizen and the nation state as a monopoly on the recognition of legitimate membership. While challenging its monopoly, denationalized citizenship occurs within the state as a legal and political framework, where the flourishing of subnational communities is recognized as a legitimate and even necessary condition for enhancing political participation and strengthening social cohesion. Within this perspective, citizenship becomes a complex web of overlapping practices (different groups call for different citizenship rights), which must be promoted at a variety of levels in order to make our belonging to very different communities compatible with the overall legal order enforced by the state.

The process of denationalization has led to a growing legal recognition of dual or multiple citizenships. This may be read as a third stage of the development of modern citizenship: the original citizenship as an irrevocable link between a given territory and the individual (one individual, one citizenship) has been replaced, with the second industrial revolution, by exclusive citizenship (one individual, one citizenship *at a time*), which is now challenged by the model of a multiple citizenship, according to which every person is *concurrently* regarded as a citizen of more than one country under the laws of a given number of states.

The quest for (and the lack of) a full integration has decisively contributed to reject, or at least to undermine, the arguments against any form of multiple citizenship. According to these criticisms, dual citizenship would eventually discourage integration, lead to serious conflicts between exclusive duties (with special regard to military service and fiscal imposition), foster a sense of belonging to different and incompatible realities and constitute a source of social inequalities between dual citizens and other people. Moreover, the countries that base their citizenship on the principle of the *jus sanguinis* – according to which a citizen is anyone born to one or both parents who are already citizens of the state – are more and more complementing it with procedures, usually reserved for second-generation migrants, based on the *jus soli* – according to which a citizen is anyone born in the territory of the state.

Most of the developed countries have undergone a similar process of *de-ethnicization of citizenship*, which has been primarily due to the need to import workers and to provide professional skills. Yet, after the development decade 1991–2001, an evident slowdown in growth has occurred. In most Western countries, in particular, the naturalization policies for immigrants – which were hitherto actively promoted as the most effective way to include first-generation immigrants (in some cases even preceded by the recognition of specific political rights) – are more and more depending on the highly discretionary management-type role played by administrative organs in establishing whether the legal requirements for acquiring citizenship have been fulfilled (minimum period of residence, no criminal record, economic and material self-sufficiency, linguistic and cultural integration).

Postnational citizenship, on the contrary, refers to practices and experiences of social sharing that actually exceed the legal and cultural framework of the nation state. In crossing boundaries, this process provides for inter-communitarian (informal transnational citizenship) as well as supranational models of membership (formal federal citizenship, as in the paradigmatic case of the European Union).

Accordingly, a different concept of the normative requirements for citizenship has emerged. Citizenship is no longer depicted as the main legal effect of political self-determination, and as such an essential prerogative of the state, but as a basic right that is intimately linked not to a circumscribed territory but to the *freedom of movement of every individual* – at least whenever a person is persecuted and deprived of basic freedoms in the country of origin (citizenship as a conditional right). As a consequence, the most critical issue is to provide an adequate justification for the criteria by which to regulate and control the influx of migrants.

The only partial (if not completely failed) inclusion of both the new migrants and the segments of the population with fewer resources to actively participate in political life has greatly contributed to shape a dual-class society, 'a family with live-in servants' (Walzer 1983: 52). What is more, even the most democratic systems appeared to be unable to prevent large-scale exploitation and marginalization of the weakest. Why did this happen? Why do minority groups tend to be systematically excluded and, more fundamentally, perceived as a minority by the dominant culture? The concept of *structural violence*, mainly developed in the 1970s, can be considered an attempt to answer these crucial questions (Galtung 1996).

The concept of structural violence extends the analysis from direct or actual violence (behavioural violence) to *indirect or potential violence*, that is, to forms of violence that do not seem to involve a perpetrator who acts intentionally. As a result, structural violence is often hard to see. Why is it defined as *structural*? Essentially, for two reasons: on the one hand, because violence is embedded in the social structure of a given interactional context (structural as essential); on the other hand, because it cannot be prevented without completely undermining the social structure as a whole (structural as necessary). The basic structure of society thus represents the means by which violence, originally perpetrated to establish the existing social hierarchy, is reinforced and perpetuated. Structural violence refers to different systematic ways – from unfair social conditions to extermination policies – in which social structures harm or disadvantage individuals by denying them access to basic goods, resources and opportunities and consequently by preventing them from developing their cultural, communication and material capabilities.

As can easily be seen, structural violence entails a concept of domination more sophisticated and complex than those that focus exclusively on the government (see 1.1.2). From the present perspective, domination occurs whenever an agent or group relegates another agent or group to a marginal and subordinated position determined by a persistent asymmetry of power (in order of increasing relevance: military, economic, political and cultural). As a result, marginalized individuals become unable to fulfil their own potential and to fully develop their personal, interactional and social skills. Within this perspective, cultural violence is conceived as the ideological legitimacy of the remaining forms of violence. On the one hand, the social roles and meanings on which the system of exploitation is based are described as legitimate/normal/self-evident. On the other hand and consequently, any protest and demand for change is pre-emptively discredited and neutralized (that is, excluded from the public discourse as non-relevant or foolish).

A few years later, with the collapse of the Eastern Bloc and the end of the actual balance of power that had characterized the Cold War era, another major change occurred. Armed force – both as an exclusive prerogative and a complex set of resources, knowledge and organizations – can no longer be said to be a monopoly of nation states. The geopolitical horizon post-1989 gets rid of the foundational oppositions that ground modern politics and modern war in particular: public vs. private, internal vs. external, civilian vs. military (Galli 2010). This is not to say that states are no longer the holders of the right to declare war (*jus belli*), but rather that their supremacy is more and more challenged by an increasing number of non-state competitors, and also more and more conditioned by an increasing number of factors other than the national interest, in favour of particular interests and small groups of people.

The emergence of new groups and factions ready and able to resort to force has led to an asymmetrical relationship between state and non-state actors, at both an international and a national level. At the international level, the possibility of entering the market of violence for a greater number of subjects has different consequences for different political contexts. At the national level, it has different consequences for different spheres of society. Let us consider these two levels in more detail.

International (or extra-communitarian) level. The concept of asymmetric warfare is frequently used to describe contemporary armed conflicts (Thornton 2007). The end of the balance of economic and geopolitical power that has hallmarked the half century of Cold War (1945–91) has led to a unipolar world, largely (if not completely, at least in the immediate aftermath) dominated by the United States, which appeared to be the only superpower. As proof, the United States accounts for 40 per cent of the entire world's defence spending. Moreover, the collapse of the Eastern Bloc has led to the possibility of waging war with almost no casualties (on the winner's side). This original geopolitical shift appears to be the real cause of the basic asymmetry of contemporary wars, that is, their being characterized (and actually resolved) *from the very beginning* by an unbridgeable gap in the means and resources available to the conflicting sides (Kaldor 1999).

But there is also an asymmetry in the way war is experienced. The new wars are confined to the territory of the weakest party. Any armed conflict that involves a world power (and mostly in the case of the United States) is far from becoming a common experience: ecological, logistic and civilian costs and consequences are born exclusively by the defeated party. It follows a very different impact on the people involved: while the civil society of the weakest state is bound to collapse, in Western countries no feature of normal economic, political and social life is suspended. A multilevel practice of risk management has greatly contributed to controlling risks of different kinds (military, economic, political). As a result the risks are generally reduced and, for the remaining part, transferred to the enemy. Unpredictability, which has always been one of the most crucial features of any armed conflict, is thus reduced to a minimum and the war itself can now be reduced to an economic variable (Shaw 2005).

Finally, there is a directly proportional relationship between the increasing gap between the two parties involved and the emergence of the new forms of terrorism adopted by the weakest party and the pre-emptive attack carried out by the strongest party. The weakest adopts unconventional strategies, such as guerrilla tactics and terrorist actions, to offset deficiencies in means and resources. The other side and consequently the strongest is forced to take pre-emptive action in order to anticipate and counter the offensive strategy of the enemy. Both sides share the belief that these unconventional strategies are for them the only viable solution to counter enemy tactics. A more expensive alternative to neutralize the superiority of the counterpart remains the development of a nuclear weapons programme, which can be considered a strategic equalizer especially for the weakest side. The distinctive character of contemporary war is thus to be viewed in the increasing adoption of unconventional strategies, such as nuclear weapons, terrorist attacks and pre-emptive actions (Colombo 2006).

National (or intra-communitarian) level. The aim of contemporary wars is not primarily the achievement of a political goal, but the maximization of private profits by single individuals or groups (factions, militias, armed gangs of very different kinds). War is thus *criminalized*, that is, waged by an increasing number of non-public actors – either absolutely (civil wars) or partially (asymmetric wars) – which are more similar to criminal organizations than to belligerent armies (Van Creveld 1991). As a result, the far-reaching consequences that continue long after war is over – transfer of capital and debts, advantages of the spoil system, new balances of power – are transferred to, and capitalized on by, private subjects and well-defined groups of people.

In a nutshell, violence is *privatized*. At both an international and a national level, the option to resort to violence is available not only to states or hierarchical organizations operating throughout the occupied territories (paramilitary forces or resistance movements) but also, especially after the decolonization process, to a multiplicity of fighting units, motivated by private interest and characterized by a non-hierarchical structure and a large degree of autonomy.

This transformation is due to four main factors. First, while during the Cold War the two blocs were forced to provide financial support to their allies and zones of influence, the drastic cuts in military spending have forced many groups of fighters to find new ways to finance their activities. Secondly, in certain contexts the collapse of the state as such has brought about the dissolution of the army. Thirdly, almost all kinds of weapons are less and less expensive and easier and easier to find and manage. Fourthly, in most cases irregular forces and paramilitary groups are in a position to offer immediate and greater earnings than regular armies. In a nutshell, contemporary soldiers are more akin to unscrupulous plunderers than to guerrilla fighters, even though they often adopt the tactics of the latter.

But the privatization of violence is not confined to 'armies without states'. State national security, in its different forms and spheres, undergoes a similar process, even in Western countries. In this second case, privatization essentially consists in a transfer of key military functions and activities from the public sector (the state) to the private sector (the market). This is mainly due to the fact that 'military force is considered a solution, or part of a solution, in a wide range of problems for which it was not originally intended or configured' (Smith 2005: xii). In brief, war – and security in general – is no longer considered to be one of the most relevant tasks of the state, but rather as an expensive set of activities that must be externalized. The increasing professionalization of armies is probably the most well-known, but not the most relevant, example of this trend.

In fact, another and more striking example is the proliferation of private military companies and societies, which offer services and expertise meant to train, complement or substitute official armed forces in the service of government (from logistics and assistance to reconstruction and highly dangerous missions in which states do not want to be directly involved). While in the First Gulf War (1991) there used to be at least 50 military personnel for every contractor, during the Second Gulf War (2003) the proportion was 10:1 (Singer 2003). The whole system of private military industry is now worth over 100 billion dollars a year and is constantly expanding. Moreover, a growing number of private security companies do not sell their services to governments but to other private companies. This practice of subcontracting decisively contributes to the removal of any effective constraint on the conduct of these companies. At the end of the first half of 2007, the number of private contractors hired by the coalition led by the United States in Iraq had exceeded the number of regular soldiers. This fundamental change has marked the beginning of a new epoch in the history of war and in its relationship with the state.

The inclusion of the private sector in the conduct of war is not without serious consequences. In fact, war is no longer conceived and waged as a zero-sum game, according to which the gain of a given party is exactly balanced by the losses of the opponent (and then A – along with its providers – maximizes its profits if and only if it defeats B, since the interests of the two parties are *mutually incompatible*). On the contrary, the interests of those private service providers turn out to be *not only compatible, but even necessary for the existence of each other* (the area bombing campaign waged by the providers supporting A is, in more than one way, the condition of possibility for the reconstruction of the destroyed highway undertaken by the providers supporting B). The gains of the private military companies, as well as those of the local militia, are thus no longer dependent on the specific outcome of the war (that is, on the victory of their respective side) but on the war as such, that is, on the indefinite perpetuation of the conflict, regardless of who will be the winner (Avant 2005). If this is true, the interests of the market and reasons for peace – as well as the interest of a relevant part of civil society and the convenience of the state – conflict with each other. Finally, this major shift marks the end of the last liberal utopia: the achievement of a perpetual and universal peace through the global expansion of a free market system.

Above the State

The key concept of the present chapter is *globalization.* Several different theories have been proposed to account for this complex set of processes and transformations, which have different dimensions and occur in very different contexts. According to some scholars, it is far from being evident that a real process of globalization is taking place. Others consider that although globalization is actually described as an ongoing process that brings about a major transformation in the way social interactions are conceived and structured, it can hardly be considered a new and emerging trend. From a different viewpoint, global processes are more likely to be the consequences rather than the causes of other prevailing global trends. Yet another perspective considers that the global age, after a period of extraordinary expansion (roughly coinciding with the two decades 1980–2000), has now entered a downward spiral, determined by those dark forces such as economic crisis and terrorism that the global process itself has, willingly or not, evoked and developed.

Obviously, a more detailed answer to the basic question 'What is globalization?' varies from author to author. Nevertheless, a minimal definition of globalization can be taken as: *the set of processes of extension, intensification and acceleration of the multilevel interdependence that binds together a growing number of social actors in their everyday interactions.*

Section 2.1 will discuss four of the most influential theories of globalization. The theories we will be taking into account focus on two questions that are key to our analysis. The first is as follows: Is the growing interdependence among the subjects involved in the global processes leading to cultural homogenization on a global scale or rather to even more differentiated societies? The second question concerns states as the main actors in the international system: Are the nation states playing an active or a passive role in this transition? Section 2.2 will emphasize how globalization is profoundly changing one of the key elements of modern politics, i.e. the coexistence and interaction between sovereign states. According to some authors, a normative and more inclusive democratic framework beyond the states is not only possible but also necessary. What is more, this cross-border extension would allow the existing liberal democracies to overcome their current crisis and even to grow much stronger. According to a more prudent approach, what is needed is simply – and more pragmatically – the implementation of inter-state policies that may promote a peaceful, if not necessarily democratic, coexistence between states.

2.1 Theories of globalization

In dealing with the two questions mentioned above, we will consider four authors who specifically focus their analysis on the different political and social outcomes determined by the relationship of interdependence between local interactions and supranational flows. The driving force of this relationship is the clash of competing and conflicting transformations, that is, of major trends that give rise to similar countertrends. The authors we are referring to are Zygmunt Bauman, Ulrich Beck, James Rosenau and Saskia Sassen.

According to Bauman and Beck, the national and the global levels are ultimately two *mutually exclusive* dimensions. The factual coexistence of the two levels in contemporary societies leads to a fragile and precarious balance that is the source of relevant parts of the pathologies (Bauman) and paradoxes (Beck) of Western democracies. If this is true, then the categories and concepts of classical social theory, based on the centrality of the nation state and the underlying processes of rationalization, turn out to be completely outdated and basically useless. On the contrary, Rosenau and Sassen describe the national and the global levels as two *deeply interdependent* dimensions that complement each other. Accordingly, social theorists must profoundly rethink, and not dismiss, the categories and concepts of classical social theory.

Before moving on, let us briefly consider the impact of the financial and economic crisis of 2007–8 on the debate on globalization, with particular regard to the relationship between political self-determination, democratic procedures and economic requirements which lies at the heart of global capitalism (Stiglitz 2002). Within this perspective, the global age, and in particular its current neo-liberal condition, has marked the end not of the state as such, but rather of the different forms and models of welfare state developed in the last century. While the essential aim of both scholars and politicians seems to be to find an acceptable – and very difficult – balance between the democratic principles and the imperatives of the market (Rodrik 2011), neo-liberal policies are actually accepted and even promoted by different subjects at different levels (Dardot and Laval 2014).

The dawn of the welfare state is the ultimate consequence of the end of the forced alliance between the capital and the democratic state, the industrial manufacturing and a wider legal-institutional system where a political compromise takes precedence over any other necessity. The basic asymmetry of contemporary societies – the overwhelming power of the market and the increasingly limited resources of the state – stems from the fact that while the state needs the market, the market no longer needs the state. This is a capital change, which is mainly due to the transition from a capitalism based on the production of money by means of commodities to a capitalism based on the maximization of the production of money by means of money. What is essential to financial capitalism is thus the subordination of production to the accumulation of money profits. Investment becomes the dominant economic function. Value is no longer *produced*, but *extracted* from the greater number of peoples and ecosystems. The essential aim of this form of capitalism is not the production of objects, but the control of society (Gallino 2011).

Yet, states and public institutions in general are far from being the predestined and sacrificial victims of the irresistible power of the market. Quite the contrary, they have *consciously and purposely* adopted over time political and legal measures – such as full deregulation of financial activities and the labour market, extensive privatization of public goods, and competitiveness as the key issue for economic growth and the main strategic goal of the state – that have decisively contributed to paving the way to the overwhelming forces of the free trade. This failure to take political responsibility is not the outcome of a political struggle, but rather the consequence of a political will: it is a retreat, not a defeat (Strange 1996). In other words, the power formerly held by the states has not been 'stolen' by profit-oriented enterprises or multinational corporations but, more often than not, voluntarily transferred to them by public institutions. The states have more and more limited their policy to organize their own decentring and transferring their regulatory powers to the global market (Sousa Santos 1995). As a matter of fact, the public intervention during what has been labelled 'the return of the state' has amounted to a full political and financial support of the markets, which were both the trigger and the remote cause of the crisis itself. As a result, (national) states sustain the (global) market, which will in turn improve (or at least it is said will improve) the economic and social conditions of the citizens. The state that is returned to the scene, therefore, is but a regulatory agency of global capitalism, which has decisively contributed to making free trade the true driving force of our times. As a consequence, the democratic institutions and legal guarantees which the state is called upon to ensure – and which constitute its distinctive characteristics as a public subject that pursues collective goals – become nothing more than an empty shell (Crouch 2004, 2011).

2.1.1 The contraposition between national and global

The basic claim of Zygmunt Bauman's theory (Bauman 1999, 2001) is that globalization does not lead to the homogenization of different lifestyles and cultures, but rather to a greater divide between two opposite social groups, a basic dualism which is extended on a global scale and which is in turn determined by the amount of material resources and concrete possibilities the two groups respectively have of moving across borders. While for a narrow group of individuals – the 'tourists', that is, the members of a transnational global elite – the increased mobility of capital, data and knowledge opens up new possibilities and lasting freedoms, at the other extreme, because of the same global process, the rest of the world – the 'vagabonds' – is confined to a passive role and totally deprived of the possibility of taking advantage of these new opportunities and thus obtaining a reasonable status in society. Tourists and vagabonds are in some ways equally free to move, but while tourists do so because they are looking for ever more satisfying consumer pleasures in the global market, vagabonds are forced to migrate to escape poverty, war, disease. While tourists are the heroes of globalization, vagabonds are its victims, relegated to live in non-places where no symbolic tie, communitarian sense of belonging or even personal identity is possible.

The main consequence of this basic divide is a disconnect between the two groups and the growing exclusion of the poorest: the greater the range of possibilities for the tourists, the worse the condition of the vagabonds. This relationship is in turn the consequence of the disconnect between economic power and social obligations that lies at the heart of the contemporary capitalist system, or – which is the same – between power, as the ability to achieve a given aim, and politics, as the ability to decide what goal must be achieved. There is no longer any (necessary) connection between profit making and the context of commodity production. What is more, for the first time in history, profits can be completely separated from externalities. The damaged environment (urban, cultural and emotional) to which the larger part of the world is condemned is thus the other side of the extraterritoriality of the considerable economic power concentrated in the hands of a global elite.

It follows that the elite that runs the world and controls the global agenda has no interest in public issues, since its means of subsistence and development are structurally disengaged from a specific local context. At the other extreme, those who are forced to flee their homes worldwide are deprived of any *effective* public forum for discussion, which was meant to provide the necessary mediation between individual and community, production requirements and contextual needs. Without this much-needed form of mediation, the top-down solutions imposed by the global elite give rise to dramatic conflicts and forms of exclusion on a local scale, which in turn lead to outbreaks of violence directed particularly against those groups thought to be the root cause of the crisis.

Contrary to appearances, the condition of the most advantaged, that of the tourists, is far from being reassuring and assured. The total lack of certainty, which is both necessarily required and ultimately reproduced by the global market, inevitably weakens any form of social membership, including that of the most exclusive groups. In fact, if they fail to cope with the demands and pressures imposed by the 'liquid life' that hallmarks the global age, the tourists can turn into vagabonds. The 'wasted life' of the powerless masses that are doomed to a ceaseless wandering is the recurring and terrifying nightmare of even the most powerful people. A generalized and continuing condition of existential precariousness and uncertainty is the distinctive and inescapable character of what Bauman defines as postmodernity.

The certainty provided by modern institutions is thus replaced by a motley array of unstable identities, forged within the context of structural violence established through radical deregulation policies by the neo-liberal forces. What is extended on a global scale is first and foremost the indeterminate, unruly and decentralized character of contemporary social transformations, which occur in a largely lawless context and in the total absence of any central authority. Within this perspective, then, globalization appears to be a set of unintended and unforeseeable casualties, an inescapable fate that is very far from the exciting and ambitious project of modernity.

This structural condition of precariousness – which is, according to Bauman, the distinctive character of the global age *par excellence* – includes more dimensions, one for each solid form of social life that has been lost: the loss of *security* (stable and reliable bonds, points of reference, institutions), the loss of *certainty* (for the choices individuals have to make in every stage of their life) and the loss of *safety* (being shielded from any danger to one's body and its extensions, that is, property, home and neighbourhood). This process results in a vicious circle. The loss of these three dimensions of stability undermines the psychological and social conditions that are necessary to conceive and carry out a collective project to tackle this condition of precariousness. We lose confidence in ourselves, then in others; this turns our daily life into a state of worry, anxiety and fear, and this condition in turn contributes to the erosion of any form of mutual trust and solidarity.

Globalization marks the end of the nation state as a socially and culturally situated community, within which individuals recognize each other as sharing a common identity and contribute to the project of a collective insurance against individual misfortune and its consequences. In this privatized society, people are reduced to individual units with no social ties. Accordingly, while the public sphere turns out to be unable to cope with basic social needs, private concerns, anxieties and frustrations are projected into the social space, with no mediation by an external or superior authority. As a result, the various demands end up being the different pieces of a puzzle that is impossible to figure out. They can be juxtaposed, but not mediated or articulated into a common social project. This shifting relationship between the public and the private spheres leads to two complementary processes, i.e. the privatization of politics and the mediatization of private life.

The spread of individual freedom in the most developed countries goes hand in hand with an increasing political impotence, which undermines social and political development. The wider the range of possibilities offered by the market, the more people seem to be dissatisfied with their lives. According to Bauman, this is due to the fact that the very pursuit of individual freedom ends up eroding and undermining those collective systems of political authority and social security that are needed for a stable life. The privatization of social security in its different forms (public order, personal formation, individual autonomy), along with the alienating effects of a radically desocialized conception of agency and well-being, is the root cause of the transition to the postmodern condition.

Modern society is a society of producers grounded on a firm institutional framework, which is called upon to assess the different relationships among its members. The postmodern society, instead, is a society of consumers based on an ever-changing set of individual desires. This transition has in some way reversed Freud's trade-off between security and freedom (or, in a wider perspective, between social order and self-expression). In the postmodern condition, individuals are willing to accept a lower degree of security in order to enjoy more freedom. Yet, at the same time, this freedom must be defended from ever-present threats of different natures (terrorist attacks, economic crises, political instability and so on). Security is reduced to the personal, physical, immediate and visible dimension, while the 'real' power appears to be impersonal, immaterial, remote and invisible. The outcome is a mix of severe repression (usually against disadvantaged minorities or deviant groups of people) and social sublimation, a practical necessity dictated by the diffuse feeling of being threatened by something undefined. As a result, the public sphere is reduced to a motley array of private worries and politics to the task of securing public order.

The modern experience of time is thus replaced by a multitude of 'eternal instants' – events, accidents, episodes – which have no connection to (a forgotten) past and (a frightening) future. The solidity of modern society turns into a maelstrom of perpetual reshaping of identities, roles and meanings. Bauman's concept of liquid societies is meant to grasp this condition of constant uncertainty and precariousness. Since the postmodern eternal present makes long-term life planning actually impossible, the intensity (rather than the extension) of life becomes the essential need of the global age. This is why consumerism – as the main source of meaning of contemporary life – is so closely linked to the alienating experience of our time. As the only service provider, the market becomes the sole legitimizing principle and yardstick for any kind of social interaction, a self-regulating and transnational social space within which individuals can be the consumers who are called upon to make their own choices and take their own risks in a highly competitive and alienating context, but who are also the commodities to be exchanged or exported (migrants, workers, refugees).

While providing a more nuanced view of how globalization may have affected our self-conception as social agents and democratic citizens, Ulrich Beck (2006, 2009) stresses, with even greater emphasis, the need for a paradigm shift in contemporary social theory. That is, political and social theory has to move beyond bounded categories of the nation state and develop a truly global approach – an analytical-descriptive perspective that Beck defines as 'methodological cosmopolitanism'.

This cosmopolitan sociology – as distinct from normative or philosophical cosmopolitanism (see 2.2.1) – is based on the inclusive strategy underlying a both/and logic, which replaces the exclusive either/or logic that lies at the heart of methodological nationalism and its founding dichotomies (above all, public vs. private, internal vs. external, political vs. civil). Owing to the increasing incongruence and the radical shifting of boundaries and levels that characterize the global age, the complex overlapping of institutional and informal mechanisms, of transnational networks and local relationships, cannot be satisfactorily accounted for in the framework of a state-centred perspective. Only such a 'cosmopolitan turn' is able to shed light on the dialectical relation between contextuality and non-locality, and on the *situated* experience of this *de-contextualizing* process, which is always mediated and interpreted *from within* a particular – that is, contextualized – point of view and a specific national society. In turn and at the same time, the view and society in question are radically challenged and transformed by this far-reaching process of cultural homogenization.

In a stunning reversal of conventional wisdom, Beck emphasizes how, far from being anything new, the (forced) mixing of cultures, views and identities, which is usually associated with globalization, is the rule in world history. On the contrary, the statehood (and in particular the nation state), which is often conceived as a sort of timeless reality, is but a three-centuries-old exception. Nonetheless, differently from the previous ones, the current forms of cultural hybridization (cosmopolitanization) are at once reflexive and caused by specific events.

What is new, then, is not the increasing interdependence of different levels of interaction and different social agents beyond national borders, but the awareness of this historical trend – that is, *its self-conscious political affirmation, its social reflexivity and its recognition before a global public opinion* (cosmopolitan outlook). Yet, this interdependence is the result of unintentional and unseen side effects of actions that were not intended as globally oriented. The increasing recognition of the risks springing from such a global interdependence (environmental disasters, terrorist threats, economic crises) – what Beck has defined as the 'world risk society', that is, a society dominated by the ubiquity of global risks that threaten the very existence of whole communities and social contexts – has finally led to the common awareness that radical reforms in global governance and the creation of effective global institutions (institutional cosmopolitanism) can no longer be postponed or put off.

The clash between the ongoing process of cosmopolitanization and the competing attempts to restore national priorities is characterized by a dialectic whose outcome is open, depending on how national and supranational institutions will deal with the challenges faced by the world risk society. Globalization is a double-edged process. In fact, every new global risk carries with it a *potential* solution to the threats it poses (above all, the very global awareness of such a risk). In other words, the greater the global risk, the greater the global awareness of the need to avoid or reduce it. In this transitional stage between the old world grounded on the nation states and the quest for new supranational institutions, the primary task of politics is no longer to take a decision, but rather *to manage the unforeseen risks and side effects* that any political decision inevitably has in the global age.

In the emerging *world risk society*, the risks, insecurities and side effects of modernization – which are mainly provoked by political decisions and not by natural disasters – know no political, social or geographical boundaries. Accordingly, while the first modernity is characterized by the production of wealth (maximum well-being at minimum risk), in the second modernity the social production and distribution of goods and opportunities is systematically accompanied by the social production and distribution of potentially catastrophic risks (minimum well-being at a maximum risk). To cope with this unprecedented challenge, the international politics based on the security of nation states as a major issue (first modernity) must be replaced by a conscious *postnational politics of risk* (second modernity), whose fundamental aim is not to determine what could be done, but rather what should never be done.

A further reason to adopt a cosmopolitan approach to global issues arises from examining the concept and trends of social inequalities, along with their transformations owing to the fact that capacities and resources actually transcend national borders. If read through the lens of a national perspective (that is, by referring to concepts such as trade unions, social classes, welfare state systems, parties and so on), social inequalities are likely to remain not only unaddressed but even unnoticed, since their most radical and relevant forms nowadays occur on a global scale. In order to handle the challenge posed by the complex relations between otherness and boundaries, Beck puts forward what he calls a *realistic cosmopolitanism*. It essentially consists in a universalist minimum that includes both inviolable substantive norms (proscriptions against violence, exploitation and authoritarian forms of governance) and binding procedural norms to deal with otherness across frontiers and to avoid, as much as possible, ideological presuppositions that risk seriously limiting the inclusiveness of this strategy. As an inclusive approach, the realistic cosmopolitanism should be a summation or synthesis of the various forms of universalism, relativism, nationalism and ethnicism adopted at the end of the first modernity. From the current perspective, these four strategies for dealing with difference and inclusion do not exclude, but mutually presuppose, correct, limit and support each other. According to Beck, this is the only way, at least in the present global age, to avoid extremism and to enhance the promotion of cultural difference within a common political framework.

2.1.2 The interpenetration between national and global

The theory of globalization developed by James Rosenau (2003, 2006) is based on what may be defined as a sociological approach to international relations. According to this peculiar perspective, while precariousness remains a distinctive feature of our times, globalization is not primarily described as a prevailing condition or a desirable state of affairs, but rather as a complex network of inter-actions that connect the micro-interactions between individuals to the macro-interactions between different organizations and states. Accordingly, the local and/or the national level should not be seen merely as a passive receptor of global inputs, but as a driving force and a strategic space for the development of the very global process (the same view is shared by Sassen).

Globalization should be essentially understood as an intricate set of interlocking relations and opposite trends that go beyond national borders and affect any social context. As a result, the tendencies toward delocalization and unification are in some way counterbalanced by the opposite tendencies toward localization and fragmentation. According to Rosenau, globalization comprises a motley array of different forces, trends and transformations that act in opposite directions. Accordingly, while all social actors (states, NGOs, transnational corporations, professional associations, ethnic minorities and knowledge communities) are increasingly mutually dependent in a variety of ways, at one and the same time this very process paves the way for the emergence of major countertrends. Given this interplay of opposite polarities, the global age appears to be marked by pervasive uncertainties, ambiguous changes and constant contradictions, whose enormous impact radically and irreversibly changes the way we experience the world.

The theory of globalization developed by Rosenau is founded on an understanding of the multilevel relationships between three complementary processes, which constitute the driving force of contemporary global changes. At the *micro-level of interactions between individuals*, the most relevant dynamic is what Rosenau calls a 'skill revolution', that is, the expanding ability of people to know their own value and perceive where their skills will be best rewarded. This leads to a more effective integration between different skills and abilities that aim at achieving a given social goal. At the *intermediate level of micro-/macro-interactions* – within which individuals both determine and are determined by the collectivities of which they are a part – a systemic interdependence involves a dislocation of power from traditional institutions to new groups – in most cases, subnational groups – that are emerging as major players in global politics. Finally, at the *macro-level of interaction between public authorities and public companies*, Rosenau depicts a bifurcation in the way global power is exercised, according to which a complex and relatively autonomous multi-centric network of informal structures has emerged as a competitor of the long-established state-centric world. This multi-centric world consists in a network of different subjects that both compete and cooperate with each other to achieve their own aims.

In turn, the interplay of these three levels and dimensions of inter-action involves three different global dynamics. The first is an endless series of *distant proximities*, that is, a network of meanings, tools and practices that are at once remote/distant and close/contiguous. The ultimate outcome of such a clash between forces pressing for greater globalization and forces promoting greater localization is a comprehensive process of *glocalization*, which emphasizes the ongoing hybridization of global trends and local experiences and the dialectical relationship between once-separated domains, fields and categories.

The second global dynamic is called by Rosenau *fragmegration* (combination of fragmentation and integration). It refers to the combination of the simultaneous integrative/centripetal forces that operate alongside with disintegrative/centrifugal forces. This ambivalent character of global trends giving rise to systemic countertrends leads to weak outcomes, precarious balances, shifting conditions and rapid changes. As a result, the same change may be perceived by some as a danger and by others as an opportunity, depending on the social context taken into account and the interpretive perspective actually adopted.

The third dynamic is the proliferation of various *spheres of authority*, whose interaction decisively contributes to the emergence of effective global governance. Every sphere – be it formal or informal – has the capacity to generate compliance on the part of those people, groups or organizations which aim at achieving a common goal. Also in this case, the effect of this global trend can be twofold: in fact, it can either empower or undermine states, as well as any other traditional form of political power. According to Rosenau, this shift in authority from (mostly) formal institutions to (mostly) informal networks of interaction marks the end of modern politics and the beginning of a new way to conceive the relations of power. Variability, contingency, anomaly and even inconsistency are the distinctive features of this global condition, which is grounded in structured and yet informal institutions supported by amorphous and yet effective interactional patterns.

The complex interplay and the unstable borders that exist between the national and the global scales is also the main focus of the sociological theory developed by Saskia Sassen (2006, 2007). The spatio-temporal coordinates of the global level are included, modified and challenged by contextual relations among different subjects. Accordingly, globalization essentially consists in a great variety of subnational processes that lead to a *de-nationalization of the national*, according to which the development of global governance neces-sitates a set of policies and political preconditions that have to be implemented in national contexts through national institutions. In a nutshell, globalization consists in the achievement of supranational aims by national means. Within this perspective, the territorial organization and institutional framework of the state (the dyad sovereignty–territoriality), far from being overcome, continue to play a key role in the global age by creating the conditions to meet the systemic requirements of the global flows (and mostly in the case of capital flows). In turn and at the same time, the development of these global flows is deeply influenced by their being embedded in the national context.

The *disassembling of the national* thus becomes the dominant condition of the contemporary world. This global restructuring and reshaping of power relations at both a national and a supranational level actually have multiple and variable outcomes. It may promote pacific integration as well as provoke violent reactions. In this regard, the development of *global cities* is a paradigmatic case. These new cities – a growing number of systemic centres that form a strategic transnational network for the global economy – is characterized by both centripetal and centrifugal forces, which may promote, alter-natively or in addition, forms of inclusion (a wider set of services and more effective forms of interaction) and/or exclusion (greater inequalities and deeper control).

The interplay of national and global processes takes the form of a multiplication of new ordering systems, based on the complex reworking of bits of territory, authority and rights (TAR). They essentially consist in partial and basic social contexts, often highly specialized, which are meant to provide specific services or to achieve strategic aims. Although they are structured within the national domain and are called upon to interact with a variety of national entities, they actually denationalize what had been constructed and experienced as national (from urban spaces to legal systems) and ultimately reorient particular components of institutions, specific practices and given forms of regulation towards global logics, namely the effective functioning of a borderless market. According to Sassen, globalization is but the space within which the different segments and dimensions of TAR coexist and interact.

The ultimate outcome of this process of denationalization of the national is the development of new jurisdictional geographies, the formation of a global capital market, the emergence of a multi-centred network of financial realities and the constituting of a global civil society mainly conceived as a global network of localized activists. All these phenomena are the complex assemblage of national components and global elements. This massive and radical redistri-bution of power on a global scale has seriously undermined both the role of governments in response to normative challenges posed by globalization and the relevance of the public sphere for promoting democracy and political accountability. Before moving on to describe the relation between order and democracy at the global level, it is worth concluding this section by considering the consequences of globalization for democratic politics.

The basic problem is the decreased ability of nationally based political systems, namely democratic regimes, to manage the conse-quences of global processes at both a national and a supranational level. This is due to two main factors. On the one hand, the global financial system imposes a series of non-negotiable political conditions and economic obligations that are often at odds with democratic principles. On the other hand, the increasing mobility of capital, stocks and labour decisively contributes to breaking the essential and historical link between capitalism and democracy – a structural condition that has ensured the sustainability of the welfare state systems in the last century (Streeck 2014). A further problem is that financial markets and global economic powers, despite their huge influence, are substantially unaccountable.

The result is *the privatization of the public sphere combined with the publicization of private resources.* In fact, on the one hand, the exercise of power on the global scale seems to require an at least partial privatization and technicization of public policy, according to which – while the executive is accepted as the sole interlocutor by the main global actors (IMF, WTO, central banks, big corporations) – legislative institutions are relegated to a secondary role (that is, to minor domestic issues) and become, at best, agents of non-representative global powers and interpreters of their commands. On the other hand, public policies and functions are increasingly transferred to financial networks and non-representative supranational institutions that impose formal and informal regulations as binding procedures for any global actor (as in the case of global governance).

Yet, as the title of the present chapter suggests, the global processes and phenomena we have considered thus far do not replace, but rather complement the state system: *above*, not *after* the state. In fact, states play a relevant role in the process of globalization as performing an essential mediating function between supranational flows and local contexts, at least with regard to the following essential aspects: implementation of treaties and enforcement of politics that support global integration; reform of welfare state systems and supervision of the privatization process; border control and regulation of migration; taxation and regulation of economic flows. Finally, and more fundamentally, it is the very reproduction of society as such to be essentially dependent on a given local context. As a matter of fact, education, research, social policies and strategic infrastructures remain firmly in the hands of the state. Without these basic services (and the institutions that actually provide them), no mediation between global requirements and local needs is possible. And without this essential mediation, any concrete and long-term global project is inevitably doomed, sooner or later, to failure.

2.2 Order and democracy in the global scenario

2.2.1 Cosmopolitan ideals and global democracy

Cosmopolitanism – which throughout Western history has always been played as an inspiring ideal (Heater 1996) – in the last decades has enjoyed a revival in the fields of moral and political philosophy (Fine 2007; Brock and Brighouse 2005). The term derives from the Greek *kosmou polites* (which Diogenes Laertius attributes to philosopher Diogenes of Sinope), that is, 'citizens of the universe'. It refers to two key notions in the conceptual horizon of ancient Greek culture: the *kosmos* (i.e. the universe or world, in a broad and comprehensive sense) and the *polis* (i.e. the city, as the basic political unit). The former is intended to signify a physical entity which, at the same time, reveals epistemic and ethical features. The *kosmos* is a complex order, characterized by an intrinsic harmony and governed by natural laws. The *polis* circumscribes the space of political action, in which the different parties of the body politic interact and cooperate. Yet, in contrast to the restricted notion of *polis* – namely the bordered space in which the political community (*koinonia politike* or, in its Latin translation, *societas civilis*) constitutes itself as a uniform body of citizens who share a political and cultural tradition – in the *kosmopolis* there are neither foreigners nor strangers and therefore no political enemies.

The very union of conflicting and, to some extent, contradictory elements – the universe, which is by definition borderless, and the city, which is by definition identified by borders meant to determine what is inside and what is outside – denotes the paradoxical character of cosmopolitanism. The basic aim of all cosmopolitan paradigms is to show that, much as politics cannot do away with differences and pluralism, it does not presuppose the conflict among distinct communities. Apart from this common premise, though, cosmopolitan theorists can be divided into two main groups: those who see cosmopolitanism as a moral ideal that has to contribute to the awareness of humans' common nature; and those who believe cosmopolitanism has to be translated into actual policies and political programmes instrumental in the erosion of the exclusionary force of national boundaries.

It is our claim that, although a few illustrious ancestors can be mentioned (the literature on the topic refers to a broad range of classics, from Zeno of Citium to Immanuel Kant), not only has cosmopolitanism risen with and within the late modern state but, even more importantly, it also advances a rethinking of the state which leaves some of its salient traits unaltered. Hence, to measure cosmopolitanism's strengths and limits it is important to spotlight its uncertain and ambiguous relationship to the state.

If many advocates of cosmopolitanism agree on the idea that social and political differences are due to historic and contingent variables, they hardly agree on what its methods and objectives should be to redress this condition of inequality. We could account for the different perspectives by means of a general and schematic (thus inevitably arbitrary) typology, based on a double distinction. As we noted above, the first and by now classic distinction is that between moral and political cosmopolitanism. This could be supplemented with a further distinctive criterion: in both the moral and the political types, some theorists believe that the main target of cosmopolitanism should be subjects (not necessarily individuals, but also groups or movements), while others maintain that institutions (states, governments, intergovernmental agencies) are the true engine of cosmopolitanism. If we apply this double distinction, we are left with four types of cosmopolitanism: moral theories targeted at subjects; moral theories targeted at institutions (see 1.2.1); political theories targeted at subjects; political theories targeted at institutions. Even though such categories are not mutually exclusive, in that they tend to overlap, this typology will help us identify the core of the various proposals and thus to pinpoint their chief differences with each other.

Moral cosmopolitanism targeted at subjects places much emphasis on the moral development of individuals and groups and claims that the successful achievement of cosmopolitan ideals is conditional upon it. Subjects, as noted above, can be either individuals or single collectivities.

Some theorists take the moral experience of the individual to be the key to the cosmopolitan project. Martha Nussbaum (1997) – in a particular phase of her thought, which she was subsequently to modify in the light of various criticisms – defines as 'cosmopolitan' those policies that are based on reason rather than patriotism or the sense of community and that therefore aspire to universalism. Nussbaum contends that the focus of cosmopolitan theories and policy frameworks should be the human being and her self-understanding. As a number of authors belonging to classic Greek and Latin composite traditions insist, according to Nussbaum cosmopolitan ideas should lead human beings to conceive of themselves as bearers of common goals and projects insofar as they are given with a common nature. Such goals and projects can be accomplished only through cooperation within a sort of Kantian kingdom of ends of rational and free beings, where each individual is always an end and never a means. She adopts the metaphor of concentric circles whereby world citizenship consists either in drawing strangers into one's own circle of affection and loyalty or in expanding one's circle so as to make it coincide with the broader circle of humanity.

Other theories targeted at subjects put not only the individual but also cultural collectivities at the core of a far-reaching moral transformation of humanity. Against communitarianism and multi-culturalism (see 1.1.1 and 3.1.1), and more generally against those who believe individual identity to be conditional upon the existence of a homogeneous substantive background, the advocates of this type of moral cosmopolitanism put forward a main thesis. They contend that every community, though seemingly uniform and homogeneous, is the product of a social construction based on political narratives (such as, for example, nationalism); if this is so, only the awareness of this element of fabrication and the openness of individuals and groups to our inescapable cultural hybridity can help today's political communities face the emerging problems of the global society.

According to Jeremy Waldron (1995) a cosmopolitan ethic is an antidote to the 'cultural exclusiveness' and 'ethnic sectarianism' which are the root cause of global injustice. In reality, Waldron argues, however profoundly one's original culture affects one's social identity, nowadays individuals belong to a variety of distinct cultural contexts and are members of many sub-state groups. In this view, cosmopolitanism should be regarded as an attempt at creating the socio-cultural conditions for the development of a cosmopolitan self who lives a freewheeling cosmopolitan life in which she enjoys a multiplicity of socio-cultural segments. Hybridity and fuzziness are not pathologies to be eradicated but precious resources for the deployment of a pluralistic democracy, where the different views of the world may be enriched and widened by the encounter with each other.

Political perspectives that look at subjects can be distinguished from moral ones in that they do not start off from a moral justifi-cation of their theoretical foundations. Rather, they by and large rely on a conventional morality condensed in the Universal Declaration of Human Rights, adopted by the United Nations General Assembly on 10 December 1948 in Paris and the subsequent International Covenants adopted by the United Nations General Assembly on

16 December 1966. This is considered to be a substantive morality, officially recognized as patrimony of the whole of humanity and thus able to integrate with a great variety of moral, cultural and religious views: if the latter are not entirely compatible with one another, they can at least agree on this basic substance and contribute to the achievement of the objectives included in these international charts. Accordingly, political versions of cosmopolitanism focusing on subjects emphasize the contradictions between the concrete activities of national governments, which seek to strategically circumvent the limits imposed on their action by human rights standards and the civil societies of the various countries, where a number of individuals and organized groups have developed a high sensitivity to the theme of fundamental rights. Based on that, the advocates of this general view believe globalization, despite its ambiguous contradictions, to be bridging the divide among local realities and intensifying the links created by the development of media and technology. This prompts civil societies to join forces to oppose illiberal and despotic regimes, hostile to the cosmopolitan ideal of a global democracy.

Mary Kaldor (1999) looks on civil society as the heart of cosmopolitan politics, in particular non-governmental organizations and independent media. Active policies of cooperation between actors at the local level and those at the international level are instrumental in the reduction of extreme localism and ethnicism, with a view to handling global problems in the light of shared universal values. Only such a struggle, Kaldor believes, will be able to prevent what she calls 'new wars', that is, wars caused by the erosion of state authorities, the weakness of representative politics and the deficits of traditional economic policies and their legal framework. In much the same vein, John Dryzek (2006) insists on the role of non-governmental organizations and of a more and more self-aware and vigilant transnational public sphere, comprised of associative and communicative networks. Cosmopolitan practices turn into incisive political actions on the part of an ideally borderless public sphere watching over the activities of governments.

Nevertheless, in our view the strongest form of today's cosmopolitanism is the political-institutional one. Unlike cosmopolitan views focused on subjects, the advocates of this type of institutional cosmopolitanism recognize that the engagement of relevant civil society organizations is an essential ingredient of the cosmopolitan recipe; yet, they contend that this engagement is likely to be fruitful only as long as national and international institutions put in place concrete reforms. The minimum common denominator of this type of cosmopolitan theories is that the state, political pivot of the last centuries, has ceased to represent the central unit of international politics and that it circumscribes a space of political action where no effective political measure can be taken. As a matter of fact, cosmopolitan theories seem to believe, decisional processes taking place at the national level are doubly unbalanced. On the one hand, the single government lacks the technical-administrative capacity to tackle global issues within its limited sphere of action. On the other hand, even though some states were able to face global issues autonomously, the decisions they would take would not be legitimized by the whole range of people who would be affected by their effects, as they would impact well outside the boundaries of the state. In short, either states are unable to solve global problems or the way they achieve that is likely to exert unpredictable and certainly illegitimate effects on a range of people much broader than the state's citizenry. Cosmopolitan theorists take this dilemma seriously and set out to delineate a political structure, above the state, where political processes might be based on a broad representation of the world population. The first step to take is the definite removal of the international system of integration – developed between the Peace of Westphalia (1648) and the Congress of Vienna (1814–15) – which represents states as unquestionable sovereign and thus as the only actors on the international scene. It is necessary to fully accomplish the ideals that inspired the constitution of the United Nations that have so far been repeatedly betrayed.

Yet, political cosmopolitans do not limit themselves to the mere (though not easily achievable) aspiration to offer guidance on how to rethink and reshape the relationships among states. Well beyond that, they claim to reconsider and revive the most valuable legacy of state politics, that is, democracy, and to pave the way for its full accomplishment – precisely because, they claim, democracy is taken out of the cramped space of state politics. On this account, the defenders of political cosmopolitanism believe that a genuine democracy can only be a global democracy.

Among other significant contributions (Brown 2009; Held 1995, 2010), one of the most intriguing formulations of democratic cosmopolitanism is Daniele Archibugi's (2008). He rethinks the relation between politics and democracy in such a way as to show that the latter requires an institutional context where its most intimate characters can unfold and prosper. Archibugi starts off from a wittingly thin definition of democracy as a regime based on the preemption of violence, popular control and political equality among citizens. Democracy is a system for the control of force (which represents a last resort) where the activities of the power-holders are constantly subjected to popular scrutiny and the citizens are endowed with an equal range of rights and duties. For Archibugi, this form of political power cannot be accomplished within the borders of one state or a system of states, for it presupposes a regime that extends beyond borders.

The route to cosmopolitan democracy, in Archibugi's model, is a complex series of gradual reforms of both the inter-state and the supra-state system, favoured by the convergence of institutions' and citizens' common efforts. This model of democracy should first of all pursue circumstantial objectives relative to specific 'areas of priority', that is, control over the use of force, acceptance of cultural diversity, strengthening of the self-determination of peoples, monitoring of internal affairs, and participatory management of global problems (such as terrorism, pandemics, pollution, poverty).

This type of institutional reform, Archibugi claims, should build on real, present-day conditions. Cosmopolitan democracy should then leave aside utopian programmes of global change (illustrated in Monbiot 2003) and look at them as a set of ideal, though noble, principles. Cosmopolitan institutions cannot be created out of nothing, for they emerge out of the consolidation of existing institutions. The pillar of cosmopolitan democracy is the strengthening of the supra-state regime of governance built on the ashes of the Second World War, which in recent decades has come to include a great number of intergovernmental and regional bodies (from the United Nations to the European Community). Yet, about the contested aim of creating a World Assembly (Marchetti 2008), that is to say, a world parliament with legislative functions, Archibugi appears much more cautious.

From this perspective, there are three levels of structural reform intervention. The first is the individual one, for a complete consolidation of human rights as a set of non-negotiable, enforceable protections. The second level is the administrative, for the construction of a global constitutionalism that may allocate powers and define competences at the global level. The third is the jurisdictional level, where supranational courts, whose decisions should be globally binding, would be required to prevent or solve disputes both among states and between states and individuals.

At the individual level, cosmopolitan democracy would endow each individual with the status of 'citizen of the world' (which would not substitute but supplement state citizenship), so as to determine and give effectivity to a basic list of rights, under the tutelage of cosmopolitan institutions. In truth, Archibugi mainly concentrates on glaring examples of violations of human rights, much less on the social and symbolic dimension of hegemony, domination and inequality. In effect, global citizenship's chief aim is to make possible, regulate and justify military intervention to protect populations from mass violence and genocide. In this reading, the individual level is strictly related to the constitutional one. In particular, it behoves the global constitution to limit and regulate the exercise of internal sovereignty, in compliance with a twofold condition: that the duty to intervene should be intended to prevent violence against the rights of the global citizens and that it cannot violate the principle of self-government. The global constitution, therefore, should contain procedures and checks to make sure that humanitarian intervention may not conceal self-interested strategies of influence. Internal sovereignty would then be safeguarded as long as it conforms with the basic provisions of human rights law, while external sovereignty would be entirely regulated by procedures meant to prevent and settle conflicts. As far as this latter issue is concerned, according to Archibugi, the activity of international courts would be vital: they would primarily carry out conciliatory, criminal and restorative functions (see 1.2.1), along the lines of the International Court of Justice and the International Criminal Court. Although the decisions of these jurisdictional bodies would be immediately enforceable, its application would be entrusted to the cosmopolitan institutions. For it should not be up to the states, as is the case at the moment, to enforce the judgement of non-state institutions, because only cosmopolitan institutions would be truly and thoroughly responsible to the whole rage of the cosmopolitan citizenry.

Cosmopolitan projects of democracy have been subject to a plethora of criticisms. The fiercest are those that regard humanitarian intervention, which all cosmopolitans by and large defend, as the diaphanous veil concealing the iron fist of neo-liberal policies (see 3.1.3). The favourable conditions that the latter aim to create would be to the advantage of the selfish actors of global capitalism more than the populations in danger (Mattei and Nader 2008). Harsh criticisms are addressed by those who draw on Carl Schmitt's critique of humanitarianism and the transformation of post-World War II international law (Odysseos and Petito 2009). These critics regard the construction of a global legal order as a way to 'criminalize the enemy' and to 'moralize war', to the advantage of self-proclaimed defenders of peace (Zolo 2002). Another, less structural and more specific type of criticism comes from multicultural and communitarian authors, who believe cosmopolitanism's weakness to lie in its aversion to national boundaries. Such a utopian inclination does not do justice to the vernacular element of politics, which is crucial to the development of situated identities and feelings of mutual solidarity.

In our view, a further nail in the coffin for the advocates of cosmopolitanism has to do with their reliance on a deep-seated political jargon that is typical of a specific, historically bounded tradition: the Western tradition. While their theoretical proposals claim to solve global problems, these are founded on quite a parochial conceptual toolkit that emerged in the wake of a well-determined history of Euro-American countries. The categories cosmopolitan democrats use are not necessarily the bearers of a blind imperialism, but they are nonetheless inspired by a well-identifiable juridico-political and socio-cultural experience. Some of the political devices of cosmopolitan theories (e.g. the sole legislator, parliamentary representation, the idea of a jurisdictional power as separate from political administration) have been elaborated in the contextual setting of Euro-American historical development and are interwoven with it, to the extent that they can hardly be as successful outside that specific geo-historical context. Moreover, democracy is presented as an endless project, as a never accomplishable approximation to an ideal; despite this, most cosmopolitan theorists offer either a thin, formal conception, which hardly grasps the link between a democratic regime and its social presuppositions, or a thick, substantial conception, as an inflexible set of civil, political and social rights that is to be fully achieved in each and every context in the same manner. In doing so, the type of cosmopolitanism on which we have mused in the last pages – the political type that looks at institutions – fails to notice how concrete legal orders and the rights that they contain constitute the outcome of the conflictual and/or harmonious relationship among social actors in a given space–time context.

2.2.2 The law of subalterns

Drawing on the considerations we exposed in the last few lines, some authors defend a different type of cosmopolitan theory that breaks the ties with the liberal and liberal-democratic legacy of mainstream Western cosmopolitanism. These authors lament the parochial nature of traditional cosmopolitanism, especially insofar as the latter builds on a conventional and somewhat myopic analysis of globalization. This is presented as a phenomenon produced in the Global North and imposed on the Global South (Rajagopal 2003; Sousa Santos and Rodríguez-Garavito 2005; Twining 2009b). Mainstream cosmopolitanism obscures the antagonistic dimension of globalization, where a growing number of social actors are engaged in a set of battles that are as minute as they are significant and disruptive. This is a set of micro-struggles around the production and application of new instruments of legal regulation (in the fields of labour, agriculture, trade, public goods), designed to promote counter-hegemonic practices within the framework of a common resistance (both symbolic and material) to the neo-liberal mantra.

The advocates of this cosmopolitanism 'from below' claim that cosmopolitan theorizing has to create a common awareness of the need to actively involve those who have more to lose than to gain from globalization (this is the case, for example, of marginalized indigenous populations, land-expropriated peasants, farmers vexed by unfavourable transnational regulations). These marginalized people should take part in forging and experimenting with a subaltern cosmopolitan legality, sensitive to the needs of the weak and the poor and released from the spell of financial and military superpowers.

This approach suggests not identifying cosmopolitanism with constitutional engineering: hardly will mere institutional reforms be able to bring about the necessary conditions for the government from below. It is, above all, necessary to discover the reasons for the blatant failure of the model of global governance favoured by the political elites of the Global North. The hegemonic, despotic character of law and politics 'from above' produces a chief, paradoxical disadvantage for the worse-off: while they are addressed as the main beneficiaries of humanitarian programmes, they are actually deprived of any chance to have a say, confined to a position of inert 'a-politicness' and hence immobilized and disempowered. This ends up as an eerie form of marginalization, which neutralizes any effort by the subject to impact on the political scenario. Clear examples of this condition are those of landless peasants who try to secure traditional land tenure against market-led tenure regimes; indigenous populations who stand up against the privatization of natural resources; the massive movement against the claimed sacredness of intellectual property.

On the same wavelength, and inspired by the basic principles of legal pluralism (see 3.1.2), other authors (Goodale and Merry 2007) understand the practice of human rights as a 'vernacularization' (that is to say, the translation into a more local dimension) of legal and political tools pertaining to human rights law. This process exerts a double effect of transformation: as a given context changes because of the introduction of these tools, so do these tools change when they are used in this context. Rarely do human rights play the same role and produce the same transformations in different geo-historical contexts, for they yield an often unpredictable multiplicity of consequences. It is therefore essential to monitor the 'process of conversion' that the application of human rights law presupposes in the here and now.

In this light, vernacularization can have two different meanings: *replication* and *hybridity*. The first consists in the transplantation of juridico-political instruments and mechanisms, produced at the international level, into different socio-cultural contexts, with scant attention to the processes of adaptation required for them to work properly. Hybridity, on the contrary, entails a deeper engagement with the local context and more attention to the way legal and political tools produced elsewhere merge with the local ones. A good example of hybridity is how women are involved in dealing with domestic violence in India, where courts intend to combine local social norms with the principles of human rights. The latter ended up merging with the values and institutions of local Indian society.

These perspectives on cosmopolitanism and human rights from below should be viewed as an invitation to take the ambiguities of international norms seriously and to decipher both their virtues and their downsides. It is necessary to assess the impact of such instruments, with an incontestably Western pedigree, and produce a weapon that is both effective in the neo-colonial war and able to mobilize resources at the bottom end of the social scale. In the Global South, the construction of macro-institutions laying down binding global decisions is by no means the only way to make human rights work. Rather, the attention of the advocates of human rights should be drawn to the micro-level of social practices that call for a scrupulous anthropological ability to discern various, concomitant effects of domination and emancipation. Against the vociferous ambition to make all human beings equal under the same law, the advocates of cosmopolitanism from below take issue with the indefinite effects of subjectification that the global techniques of government produce at the local level: if they are not just instruments of an evil, imperialistic machinery, because they endow the worst-off with concrete means to engage in socio-political battles, the voracious tendency of these means to transform those who use them must be scrutinized step by step. Only in this way will it be possible to trigger more inclusive dynamics of political participation that are able to turn the growing disaffection and political apathy into active agonism, with an eye to giving voice to the weakest and the subalterns, left at the margins by the traditional models of representative democracy (Butler, Laclau and Žižek 2000).

2.2.3 Back to the state?

If Zeno and Kant are the tutelary deities of cosmopolitanism, they are opposed to a broad range of eminent authors, from Thucydides to Niccolò Machiavelli and Thomas Hobbes, tenaciously averse to all utopias. These authors reject ideal-normative speculations and assign political theorizing analytic and descriptive tasks. Theory must take issue with the structural vices of human nature and the tendencies and counter-tendencies of historical patterns: there is no evidence to conclude that humankind is on its way to a peaceful and orderly state of affairs. In the twentieth century, such a burdensome legacy was received and developed by the advocates of 'classical realism', such as Raymond Aron, Edward Carr, Reinhold Niebuhr and Hans Morgenthau, and advocates of 'neo-realism', such as Hedley Bull, Robert Gilpin, Robert Keohane and Kenneth Waltz.

Despite numerous differences, these authors agree on a basic idea of human nature and the relation among human beings: since the latter are self-centred animals, who first and foremost aim at securing conditions of security and prosperity, they cannot but perceive relationships with others as interferences and mutual limitations. Egoistic passions and self-interest leave no hope for enduring cooperation and the constant pursuit of the common good.

Although shorn of selfless inclinations, politics is, however, the principal instrument (vis-à-vis, for example, religion and economics) to govern society. The pre-eminence of the political is vital to the existence of a safe and stable platform on which social life can develop its multifold articulations. Nonetheless, by and large all the authors mentioned seem to hold a dichotomous view of politics: whereas the organizational machinery of the state and its monopoly on power succeeded in taming the conflicts triggered by humans' egocentric inclinations, outside the state politics cannot be but a series of conflictual relations based on decisive power differentials. Therefore, at the level of supra-state politics – where the state continues to be the fundamental unit – the main objective is and should be to restrain violence and reduce the risk of conflict. A point of reference for neo-realists is Kenneth Waltz (1979), who describes states as structural units within complex international political systems. These systems are comprised of (and thus can be distinguished in the light of) three elements: 1) the existence of an ordering principle, according to which the system can be more or less anarchical and more or less hierarchical; 2) the specification of functions of formally differentiated units, whereby single units can be functionally similar or differentiated; and 3) the distribution of capabilities across those units.

If this model helps explain and map the inner structure of states, international relations are characterized by a horizontal order, among the units there is no functional differentiation and, finally, states differ in their ability to accomplish their tasks. In this framework, units are forced to rely on self-help to protect their sovereignty and national security. This anarchic scenario, however, is not tantamount to violence and disorder. On the contrary, like free enterprises in the free market, spontaneous regulation is the primary source of integration. Hence, the main variable of every international political structure is the distribution of resources among the various units, which can eventuate in either multipolar or bipolar alliance systems.

Waltz believes that a bipolar system is more stable and durable, because in a multipolar one competition is fiercer and uncertainties about the comparative capabilities of states increase as numbers grow. As a consequence, estimates of the cohesiveness and strength of coalitions are much harder.

Hedley Bull's (2002) still topical book, *The Anarchical Society*, originally published in 1977, has famously launched the idea of a 'new Middle Ages', synonymous with a polycentric society where the monopoly on sovereignty is unthinkable. Although the social setting where he was situated was notably different from the contemporary one, Bull foresaw a state of things where states, internally fragmented, try to integrate into broader units so as to transfer sovereignty to a higher level of administration. At the same time, transnational corporations and global semi-public organizations augment their influence and capacity to pursue objectives other than the ones of national governments and intergovernmental agencies. Bull's analysis brings out the ambiguities of many processes that were destined to intensify in the wake of globalization: the waning of deep-seated distinctions such as public/private or state/non-state bespeaks a deep institutional crisis that in the last centuries, at least at the level of domestic politics, had allowed the stabilization of peace and security. In substance, the end of the state, as well as the collapse of the conditions of peace and order that only the state can secure, could be conducive to a scenario of endless international conflicts. This is why Bull's prophetic words could well fit the retreat to into the state that seems to characterize the international politics of a post-financial crisis scenario, where states shy away more than ever before from the idealistic rhetoric of cosmopolitanism.

An interesting revision of the realist paradigm, which to some extent relativizes the role of the state, is structural realism. Its defenders agree with realists and neo-realists that politics has and must have the upper hand in the governance of social dynamics and that the state at present continues to be the principal actor in the international setting. Yet, structural realists claim to identify and overcome a few ingenuities of other realist schools. Barry Buzan (1991) questions the concepts of internal security and external insecurity and shows that the state is hardly capable of protecting security, in that it is variously dependent on a series of complex interactions among states. If by 'anarchy' we mean the absence of an overarching government, there can be two types of anarchy: an immature one, characterized by the struggle of individual units to survive automatically, leading to a balance of power and the reproduction of the anarchic structure; or a 'mature' version of this anarchic system, where peace and security would stem from a context of political fragmentation and ongoing, balanced, regulated interaction among states. In this latter scenario, security is no longer a Hobbesian state of affairs where one's life is safeguarded and contracts executed on account of a common, threatening sovereign. For Buzan, security is the interaction of multiple factors operating in different sectors (political, military, economic, societal and environmental), so much so that the very idea of national security turns out to be a 'systemic' security. In such an integrative perspective, where individuals, states and the international system all play a part, security is a much more complex problem than the traditional realist view believed.

In an even more sophisticated and broader theoretical framework, Barry Buzan and Richard Little (2000) insist that the theory of international relations advanced by realists and neo-realists offers an impoverished understanding of international systems, implanted in a crystallized vision of the European system of states of the modern age. This narrow understanding prevents an accurate account of the differences among systems as well as of the structural transformations and evolutions at the root of the transition from one system to another. According to Buzan and Little, the very theory of international relations must be supplemented with the history of the world and extended beyond the limits of the Westphalian system.

Although the one that emerges at the end of the Middle Ages constitutes a particular system of international relations, on account of the unit that characterizes it (the state), a diachronically more elaborate approach would be conducive to more refined and reliable analyses. First of all, international systems can be distinguished with reference to different aspects; contrary to realists' and neo-realists' insistence on the pre-eminence of political and military factors, as noted above, environmental, societal and economic variables are crucial to characterizing a system. Secondly, systems are analysed in the light of the degrees of exchange and communication among the units, which turn out to be essential to the nature of the interactions among them: conflict, diplomacy and trade. This more dynamic vision of the relation among units opens up to a reconfiguration of the role of the state as a transitory unit within the systems, whose structure evolves in response to a dynamic that cannot be entirely under the control of the single units.

Without the State

The theories examined in this chapter by and large agree on a fundamental tenet: as the mediatory function of the state is vanishing, new mechanisms of representation and integration have to be devised. Accordingly, while the conventional dyad sovereignty/government is being torn apart, the law on the one hand and the market on the other are believed to be more adept at tempering the conflicts among groups, although their centrifugal forces impinge on the ties between the states and their citizenries. In keeping with this tendency, sovereignty is being redistributed among a multiplicity of semi-autonomous sectors, while governmental tasks are reinterpreted as the capacity to self-organize.

Section 3.1 will explore a set of proposals for the reconfiguration of Western political structures that provide guidelines on how to accommodate the rise of claims to political and legal autonomy on the part of a variety of non-state actors. In doing so, we will address the issue of pluralism and its different nuances in order to tackle the question of what is really undergoing a process of progressive disentanglement from the state: are they ethnic and/or religious groups? Or are they specialized sub-sectors, such as multinational corporations and private financial agencies? Section 3.2 will show the way the different rationalities of the law and the market prove instrumental in the consolidation of sectors that are able to self-organize and to escape state control. Based on this, we will illustrate how the ethno-cultural element in many geo-historical contexts is being distorted by the encounter between extra-state regulations and neo-liberal policies, whose effects make group identities depend on the logic of the market and erode their genuine claims to autonomy.

3.1 The twilight of the only legislator

3.1.1 Multicultural politics

As early as the beginning of the twentieth century, the term 'culture' became a key concept in many fields of study (Kuper 1999). It denoted a basic, ultimate and irrefutable form of belonging: individuals are first and foremost members of a given social context that transcends and pre-exists them. Culture was regarded as the source of the self: therein individuals become subjects, that is to say, they get familiar with being situated and inherit a specific mode of interaction with their environment. If from the middle of the seventeenth century the term 'civil' signposted the capacity of human beings to clamber out of a condition of primitiveness, in the twentieth century terms such as 'culture' and 'civilization' broke their age-old ties with the concepts of progress and development. 'Culture' came to denote a 'form of life', an ensemble of epistemic and practical criteria (that is, a set of meanings and models of conduct) that cannot be compared with those of other cultures, for these ensembles are so different from each other that they are utterly incomparable. Culture turned into a term that can never be thought of in the singular: only culture*s* exist. As the idea of an inner relationship between culture and progress was replaced by the idea of a deeper connection between cultures and 'world views', so did the notions of scientific knowledge get altered. No kind of knowledge can be aseptic, universal, neutral, in that every form of knowledge is intertwined with the intuitions and beliefs in which it is rooted. In other words, 'knowledge' became synonymous with 'understanding'. As a consequence, in order for one to understand another's culture, she has to capture its core meanings, inscribed in the practices of everyday life. Such meanings, however, can be grasped only provided that one comes to share the intuitive grammar mastered by the members of this culture.

Nonetheless, from the very outset this understanding of the term culture has aroused disagreeing reactions. On the one hand, the stress on the cultural element brings to light the *ancestral and foundational character* of community life, out of which individuals are nothing but isolated atoms dispersed around the globe. In this sense, a culture is a set of beliefs, values, modes of organization, aesthetic canons, technical-technological resources, which provide human beings with a 'second nature'. Cultural practices allow fragile and instinctively deficient animals, as human beings naturally are, to leave their precarious conditions and to overcome their physical and biological deficiencies. On the other hand, however, in the same fields where culture had been adopted as a core subject matter, many critics pointed out that culture has no genuinely *natural* connotations: culture is a human artefact. In this respect, critics made two main points. First, the portrayal of culture as a homogeneous totality of meanings and models of conduct stems from the projection of those who observe from 'an external point of view' the activities of alien social collectivities. Observers tend to emphasize homogeneity and to minimize differences and thus social collectivities get objectified and (at least partially) misinterpreted. Accounts given from an external point of view fail to notice the polychromatic and multi-layered nature of every context of human sociality. The second point stressed by critics, above all by the advocates of so-called 'cultural studies', is that cultural analysis should get rid of its conservative traits to be part of a general critique of domination and hegemony, in the light of which cultures turn out to be the expression of cultural elites and high classes (During 1999). On this view, the study of cultures should be instrumental in unmasking, contesting and undermining those people and groups who use culture as an instrument of domination meant to subjugate populations and to marginalize rebellious minorities.

There is little doubt that the term 'culture' still plays a strategic role – unlike others, such as 'class' or 'superstructure', which seem not to fit the dynamics of a global world – to the extent that it opens up new fields of inquiry. Most probably its success is due to the fact that in recent decades the theme of multiculturalism (not without some distortions) has been taken as an effect of the comeback of religion in the public sphere. Culture and religion have been increasingly regarded as two sides of the same coin. Some authors – like Samuel Huntington (1996), who famously depicted the post-Cold War scenario as a clash of civilizations – have pushed it so far that they have come to identify the borders of a given culture or civilization with the borders of the religion shared by the majority of its population. Such a theoretical attitude has even accentuated the vagueness and inadequacy of the conceptual framework implanted on the notion of culture. In order to show that cultures or civilizations are homogeneous totalities, constructed around a few shared elements, some theorists have bracketed off the many differences that hallmark the various geo-historical contexts.

Despite this overextension of the notion of culture, theorists who insist on the cultural salience of religion make a point. They rightly point out that the issue of a failed secularization and of a re-sacralization of society in the global era has to do with the failure of the liberal state as a secular institution. Whereas some key political theorists engage in far-reaching analyses of the process of secularization and its impact on the political sphere of Western societies (Taylor 2007), 'post-secular' has no fixed, unequivocal meanings (Backford 2012). On the one hand, there are those who make the radical claim that secularization (that is to say, the process whereby religion was progressively expunged from the public, political realm, to be confined to the private sphere of individual beliefs) was nothing more than an ideological ploy implemented by rationalist, enlightened elites (Hadden 1987; Morozov 2008). On the other hand, other scholars make the weaker claim that the post-secular doesn't express the comeback of religion in the public, but rather signifies a change of mind in those who believed religions to be the remnants of a bygone past (de Vries and Sullivan 2006). In this latter sense, the post-secular can even be seen as a continuation of the Enlightenment by other means, to the extent that the prefix 'post' does not imply a disposal but an ongoing relationship with the tradition of secularism (Caputo 2001).

Be that as it may, there is no doubt that a big shift has occurred, which brings religion to bear on the current political scenario. The telling definition of secularization offered by Ernst-Wolfgang Böckenförde (1991) – the withdrawal of an institution from ecclesial and spiritual observance and control – is meant to point out that the modern replacement of God with the ideal of nationhood was doomed to cause havoc once nations would reveal their fictitious and transient nature. The secular state, according to Böckenförde, was unavoidably forced to rest on external supports, since it was incapable of setting out the conditions for its stable reproduction. Whereas every political community necessitates solidarity bonds that prompt people to jointly contribute to the common good, the process of secularization ended up eroding these bonds. Although in opposition to what he calls 'Böckenförde's theorem', Jürgen Habermas explains that what the state was able to overcome – the disastrous consequences of confessional wars – may make a comeback (Habermas et al. 2010). Religious wars today are being repeated not only between the secularized Global North and Islamic terrorism, but also within liberal societies. In Habermas's view, this risk should prompt liberal democratic states to even up the unfair asymmetry in the obligations they impose on religious and non-religious citizens, especially when it comes to justifying claims within the public sphere.

He thinks that a mutual learning process is likely to emerge out of this predicament. On the one hand, religious citizens and organizations are required to grant full recognition to the public sphere as a venue where no religious beliefs can be foisted upon anyone. On the other hand, secular institutions should cease forcing religious citizens to reframe their claims in a non-religious language and recognize that religious utterances can make a meaningful contribution to clarifying controversial questions of principle.

Apparently the process of globalization has successfully brought religion 'beyond secularization' (Casanova 1994) and has taken it out of a private/subjective dimension – the dimension that, according to most scholars, had long represented the iron cage of religion within the secular state. The issue of a reviviscence of religion and its political import is heightening the crisis of domestic juridico-political orders and in particular one of their pillars, namely representation. In addition, new actors enter the scene of politics and carry with them the weight of collective identities that are not entirely compatible with the traditional view of citizenship as individuals' direct relationship to state institutions. Such emerging contradictions exert a theoretical effect as they induce many advocates of multiculturalism to overhaul its conceptual framework in order to accommodate a much more complex and multifaceted reality, where both culture and religion play a renewed political role. In effect, the moment the state's claim on the monopoly of legitimate authority is being eroded by a multiplicity of bodies, minority groups within national states seize on the failure of secularism and emphasize the connection between sharing a common religion and abiding by a common (religious) law. Based on that, religious groups lay claims to jurisdictional and political autonomy.

It is in this framework that Ayelet Shachar (2001) tries to unravel the 'paradox of multicultural vulnerability': if it is true that the growing political relevance of religious groups cannot be neglected, the question to be tackled is the potential conflict between the jurisdictional autonomy of religious and cultural groups and the rights of intra-group minorities. Shachar contends that, in the light of the traditional binary view 'either your culture or your rights', the enhancement of the former is believed to hamper the latter. According to this dichotomous view, if today the state is forced to relinquish part of its traditional power to sub-state groups, the rights of vulnerable people *within* groups are put in danger, while the chances of conflicts *among* groups are increased. Such revisions could even favour those intra-group factions that are more organized and jeopardize inner dissent. Shachar points out that this misleading view pits liberal citizenship against multicultural citizenship: the former endows individuals with an equal set of rights and duties, while the latter regards subjects as having a special tie to their native group, which in turn grants them a (sometimes narrower) set of rights and duties.

Shachar elaborates a solution that aims to overcome this seeming opposition and to turn it into a resource for liberal politics. It comes down to the model of 'joint governance' where three main actors interact: the state, the group and the individual. As we will see, in Shachar's view this solution is open to taking minority claims seriously but at the same time does not put internal dissenters in jeopardy. In this regard, Shachar espouses a strong multicultural approach, based on a rather organic view of groups and their inner dynamics, much as she recognizes that members often belong to different groups at the same time. In other words, Shachar thinks of groups – or what by drawing on Robert Cover (1983) she calls '*nomoi* groups' – as religiously defined groups of people who share a comprehensive world view that extends to creating a law for these very groups. She sees this definition as applicable to other types of minority groups (ethnic, racial, tribal) insofar as their members share a comprehensive and recognizable world view that involves a specific law, along with common traditions, history, memory and conventions.

Before we delve into Shachar's proposal, it is worth mentioning the possible variants she summarizes in terms of constitutional engineering, advocated by different multicultural theories in recent years. A quick analysis of these variants will serve as a useful synopsis of the multicultural debate in the past two decades.

Shachar singles out and discusses four models.

'Federal-style accommodation' allows the division and sharing of power between different groups, in such a way as to preserve the autonomy of groups and at the same time to maintain a common political framework. However, this model presupposes that groups are territorially distributed so that precise boundaries among them may be drawn. Only within these boundaries would groups be legitimately allowed to exercise their autonomous powers. Yet, this very distribution sets the limits of the model at stake: not only does it run the risk of reinforcing the rigidity and closure of geographically stable groups, but in addition it takes no notice of trans-territorial groups whose members are tied by traditions and customs, with no need to reside in the same geo-spatial context.

'Temporal accommodation' connects institutional adjustments to specific and circumstantial issues, that is, some aspects of life that turn out to be key to the existence of a group (such as conjugal life and education). In these specific cases groups hold legitimate authority, but outside them individuals remain subject to state law. Yet, there is a problem with both what kinds of issues are to be regarded as key and the necessity to define the precise temporal periods involved.

'Consensual accommodation' sees the jurisdictions of state and groups as plainly separate, but leaves it up to individuals to opt for one of them. This model could thus be considered as a felicitous junction of liberal-democratic requirements and multicultural claims: if group members are left free to choose, state and groups are likely to engage in a virtuous competition to increase the number of members. This model, however, ends up in a deadlock. First, members could be exposed to pressures by their original groups. Secondly, individuals can hardly be knowledgeable enough to fathom the consequences of their opting for one of the alternatives. Thirdly, the state could hand over any responsibility as regards the protection of those who opt for the group's jurisdiction and thus could choose not to exert any control over the internal life of groups.

'Contingent accommodation' is a model such that the state grants autonomy to groups in specific sectors only as long as these groups see to it that certain state-defined minimal standards are met. If a group fails to do so, the state may legitimately reduce the scope of the group's autonomy. This model seems to be able to square the objective of getting more autonomy with a growing socio-economic emancipation, in that groups are prompted to foster healthy measures of competition both with other groups and with the state. The definition of basic standards would enhance cooperation between the group and the state to the advantage of members: the state entrusts groups with tasks and meanwhile monitors them; groups exert authority and create the conditions for the self-development of members. This model is, however, affected by a few flaws: Who is responsible for determining the standards to be achieved? Could these standards be used by the state to blackmail groups? Is there the risk of modifying the identity of groups when they are required to yield to the values promoted by the state? Could this model confer far too extensive powers of review on the state, so much so that it may cause serious discrimination in the exercise of such regulatory authority?

As we noted before, Shachar advocates an alternative model, joint governance, which puts emphasis on the strengths of the models examined so far, but at the same time seeks to fill in their gaps. Joint governance aims to foster a 'transformative accommodation', one that expands the autonomy of groups (understood as the exercise of legislative and judicial powers, whereby groups can freely enforce their own normative order) while ensuring that vulnerable individuals and internal dissenters are provided with effective legal tools to act against abuses. Such a profound adjustment should be structured on different types of authority operating along a horizontal axis, rather than a vertical one: this should amount to a dialogue among non-monopolistic power-holders, to which individuals could be subject on the basis of a free choice. Single individuals would then be allowed to abide by the normative regime attached to their traditions and customs, but at the same time they would remain always free to opt out when some of the measures adopted by the group prove detrimental or unsatisfactory.

Shachar bases transformative accommodation on three main principles: the 'sub-matter' allocation of authority, the 'no monopoly' rule and the establishment of clearly delineated choice options.

While in the traditional form of political organization some key issues (such as education, family law, criminal justice, immigration, resource development and environmental protection) are thought to be internally indivisible into 'sub-matters', according to the sub-matter allocation principle they are indeed divisible and can be allocated along sub-matter lines. For example, Shachar comments, in the context of marriage, there are at least two sub-matters at stake: the 'demarcating function' regulating the change of one's marital status; and the 'distributing function' covering the definition of the rights and obligations that married spouses are required to honour. The distinction between these sub-matters parallels the key legal aspects of marriage and divorce, that is, status and property relations. These sub-matters, Shachar goes on to say, can actually be governed by complementary authorities.

The autonomy of groups on specific sub-matters, Shachar clarifies, is not tantamount to a monopoly. Neither the state nor the groups would be allowed an exclusive control of the social space where these issues develop. In fact, the second principle of joint governance, the 'no monopoly' rule, recognizes the potential rivalries between jurisdictions over legal sub-matters and accordingly makes room for the intersections of multiple affiliations. Neither the groups nor the state can exert exclusive control over a contested social arena that affects individuals both as members of their groups and as citizens. In this way, the various centres of authority are prompted to operate in an institutional setting where their powers are permanently constrained. This represents an important feature of transformative accommodation: it creates incentives for both state and groups to better serve individuals, as neither of them can retain exclusive authority over individuals with multiple affiliations. This means that both state and groups must devise and cultivate ways of appealing to and attracting individuals.

To achieve that, however, the third principle must be implemented, that is, the establishment of clear-cut choice options. Individuals are allowed to choose between state jurisdiction and the group jurisdiction. They can choose to remain within the sub-matter jurisdiction of the original group ('approval') but can defend themselves against the group jurisdictional authority at predefined reversal points ('disapproval'). These options, according to Shachar, throw new light on the traditional way of understanding group membership. While traditional models only allow membership to be entirely in or entirely out, clearly demarcated and selective 'entrance', 'exit' and 're-entry' options significantly empower individual members to the detriment of dominant power-holders.

If this is so, then the strong point of such accommodation is, Shachar believes, the fact that it triggers a transformation within groups, in that members who feel dissatisfied or even abused about specific sub-matters can resist group jurisdiction and turn to the state jurisdiction. Such a virtuous movement would be able to create conditions for vulnerable members to bring into question traditional jurisdictional settings by voicing specific demands as to specific sub-matters. Joint governance should then be conceived as a three-dimensional space with three main actors, the group, the state and the individual, who simultaneously interact on different planes and in different areas.

Anne Phillips (2007) brings to light the ambiguities of Shachar's approach. First and foremost, the latter's depiction of *nomoi* groups appears to be affected by a main theoretical incongruity: How can a group embedded in an all-encompassing cultural and legal understanding of the world act as rational calculator when it comes to competing with the state about the number of constituents? Moreover, Phillips points out that Shachar's model – the core of which is the exercise of a selective exit and re-entry option – places the entire burden on individuals, with the consequence of relieving both the group and the state of any responsibility for promoting change. From this point of view, the crux of the matter is not whether or not individuals should have the right to exit, but whether or not such a right is an effective tool to protect vulnerable individuals. Indeed, Phillips argues, such an approach to multiculturalism underestimates the power of culture. While exit can hardly be seen as an easy way to get oneself out of the influence of one's original group, staying cannot hastily be taken to be a genuine manifestation of acceptance.

The right to exit is highly overestimated, as too often its advocates fail to consider that people may find it very difficult to live outside their original group: exit from a culture might entail not having any culture at all. In this regard, Shachar and more generally those who defend strong multiculturalist views make a twofold mistake. On the one hand, they implicitly hold that all those who decide to stay *ipso facto* express their acceptance. On the other hand, they take it for granted that individuals who dissent are free to leave and to enjoy an entirely new life (or at least to exit partially, as in Shachar's proposal). Nonetheless, Phillips argues, one cannot be sure that a group, in order to deter people from leaving, rather than enhance the quality of living conditions resorts to psychological pressure or to physical threats, and thus obtains acceptance coercively.

To summarize her criticism, Phillips asks four key questions that a variety of multicultural proposals fail to answer. Is there anywhere else for people to go? Do people have access to the minimal resources without which they hardly have any chance to leave? Is the cost of leaving set unacceptably high? Is it possible for people even to conceive of going out of their cultural group? Phillips argues that the first two questions, which many critics of multiculturalism have raised, bring up sensible issues. Often individuals who leave a community are forced to give up and sacrifice most of their affective and material resources. Yet, the variables that truly make exit unfeasible have to do with the last two questions, that is, the cost of exit and the possibility of conceiving alternatives. First, exit imposes costs that are neither only nor primarily financial: sometimes the costs of leaving one's community are much more of a moral type (this is the case, Phillips exemplifies, of excommunication for Catholics) that cannot be translated into financial terms, and yet could be excessively high for believers. Secondly, and more importantly, members who have interiorized the canons, values, models of conduct and criteria of judgement of their group can find it difficult even to imagine alternatives. The situatedness of members draws the contours and sets the boundaries of the frame of significance within which they perceive something as possible and/or desirable.

Based on this analysis, Phillips levels a criticism at all those perspectives that view the enhancement of a group's authority as a viable way to accommodate multicultural claims. She avers that groups tend to consolidate and strengthen their borders when the state promotes policies that portray them as organic and homogeneous entities. Paradoxically, groups' identities get reified by strong multicultural policies, based on a substantive notion of culture.

Political and judicial measures that reinforce the group's regulatory power also reinforce the relative position of traditional power-holders and heighten the despotic nature of their authority. Rather than groups, Phillips contends, rights must always address individuals. Multicultural dilemmas, in this view, should be primarily understood as general problems of democratic-constitutional states: a solution to them can be found through discussion and dialogue, where people with different cultural backgrounds talk to one another and explain the reasons why they favour particular laws or practices. In doing so, people are likely to develop negotiation skills that allow them to reach workable compromises. In summary, Phillips claims that too often cultural difference is believed to be greater than it is in reality. The path to political accommodation of difference, therefore, is a multiculturalism *without* culture that refuses to straightforwardly mirror the existing distribution of groups and favours transition and commixture.

Seyla Benhabib (2002) also voices serious doubts about Shachar's proposal. Her primary concern is with the risk that joint governance may provide solutions at a purely jurisdictional level. This model of accommodation could be detrimental to the *political* aspect of social life, one that really prompts groups to engage in discussions and debates within a common discursive arena. The re-feudalization that joint governance is likely to cause could perhaps be conducive to a non-conflictual coexistence among robust power-holders, who would be able to bring about general conditions of order and peace. Nonetheless, according to Benhabib, this model runs a serious risk: if the authorities of existing groups collapsed, the consequence would be the Balkanization of society and the emergence of new conflicts whereby new groups would compete to gain control over individuals and to acquire even more autonomy.

The solution to ethnic conflicts, according to Benhabib, should be inspired by a deliberative approach, or rather by the principle that political decisions, insofar as they want to be fair and effective, should be the outcome of extensive debate, in which all affected people may take part and have a say. From this vantage point – although she claims she is well aware of the impact of culture on perceptive categories and criteria of judgement – Benhabib puts at the heart of her model individuals rather than groups, much as individuals might belong to a group by birth or consent. In fact, liberal states cannot neglect their duty to protect the equal liberties of individuals and to ensure fair distribution of political and social rights. This makes them responsible for the resolution of problems created by cultural conflicts through an inclusive and open debate within the public sphere (that is, the broad arena comprised of actors, generally non-institutional and even informal, such as newspapers, televisions and intellectual circles). This discussion should take place in compliance with the following principles: 1) *Egalitarian reciprocity*: individuals have the same right to have a say, irrespective of the group to which they belong; 2) *Voluntary self-ascription*: individuals are free to choose whether to belong or not to their original group or to any other group; 3) *Freedom of exit and association*: the state has to measure and balance the formal and informal costs of an individual leaving a group, such as informal exclusion or ostracism or formal loss of property.

In reality, as our analysis has so far shown, it seems that multicultural theorists are not capable of unravelling the dilemma that opposes group rights both to the authority of the state and to individual rights. Although in most multiculturalist perspectives the state continues to be the key political actor, the criticisms addressed to them emphasize the risk that a multicultural accommodation of society might jeopardize the overall project of the modern state. At the end of the eighteenth century, the state emerged as the disposal of medieval and early modern particularism, that had long allowed the various guilds, associations, brotherhoods, confraternities and corporations, and even whole regions, cities, monasteries, to retain political and judicial autonomy *vis-à-vis* the different political centres (the pope, the king, the emperor), who enjoyed thin legislative and regulatory powers. The multilayered institutional framework that came to life between the end of the Middle Ages and the eighteenth century was quite a complex political and juridical organization, deliberately based on difference: in accordance with the *legal particularism* that hallmarked this juridico-political setting, individuals were not equal citizens of a common body politic, but members of specific groups, to which they belonged either by birth (men, women, nobles, peasants), or by shared faith (Catholics, Protestants, Jews, Muslims, atheists), or by profession (artisans, jurists, clerics). As a consequence, it could often be the case that a Catholic peasant and a Jewish merchant, living in the same territory, were subject to entirely different bodies of law. In other words, there were many semi-autonomous jurisdictions, with which the modern state did away through long and complex juridico-political processes known as *codification* and *constitutionalization*, along with the cutting-edge invention of *legal personhood* (that is, the principle whereby single individuals are equal before state law, in that they have an unmediated relationship to the state, regardless of their sex, religion or wealth). According to many critics, a strong multicultural approach, like the one advocated by Shachar, could endanger this equality and harm the state's primary duty to guarantee basic conditions of equality.

3.1.2 The plurality of orders

So far we have seen that multicultural projects are affected by an inborn flaw: they cannot, or do not want to, get rid of statehood once and for all, but propose recipes for the reallocation of legal and decisional powers. Shachar's theory proves the most courageous and innovative: she insists on the urgent need to create sub-authorities, partially autonomous, whose members can make informed choice, case by case, on specific sub-matters. As we have shown, however, the accommodation she advocates could engender a re-feudalization of society, as it may bring back the state of affairs that the modern state has jettisoned over the course of the past three centuries.

The approach of those who work in the field of so-called 'legal pluralism' (Tamanaha 2008; Twining 2009a) seems to be different. Based on historical, philosophical, sociological and anthropological studies, these scholars (or at least a vast majority of them) break the ties with the paradigm of the state. The strength of this approach is precisely that they rely on a theoretical framework that is not affected by the ambiguity examined above: they do not aim to find a compromise between the reasons of liberal democracy and the claims of new actors in the political scenario. Rather, they aim to show how the fractures affecting contemporary liberal states are due to constitutive malfunctions and deficiencies, which require the development of alternative models.

According to the authors we will examine, the whole project of modern statehood was implanted on a both pervasive and feeble ideology. The state of the past two centuries aimed to promote an idea of society and politics that to a great extent is mere fiction. As seventeenth- and eighteenth-century natural law theorists took the idea of a state of nature as their basic theoretical keystone, so did the state aspire to present itself as the only producer of law, order, peace and safety, that is to say, as the indispensable condition of human sociality, short of which there is nothing but chaos.

To sketch a map of the various models in the field of legal pluralism we need to bring to light its twofold matrix, so as to distinguish and classify its ramifications.

A *first type of legal pluralism* is based on a *historical-reconstructive approach*, which follows two main paths: some pluralist authors concentrate on the bumpy trajectory of European societies and the analysis of their juridico-political forms; others study the relations between the law of indigenous populations and the law of colonial minorities as a result of the processes of colonization, whereby Western states subjugated whole continents or at least part of them.

The *second type of legal pluralism* is based on both a conceptual deconstruction of prevailing jurisprudential models and a socio-anthropological analysis of forms of organization developed by non-Western populations, who were once defined 'primitive' (not in a necessarily degrading meaning) and today are commonly called 'indigenous'.

These two types of legal pluralism are often intertwined, as historical investigation rests on sound conceptual grids, while theoretical analysis rest on socio-historical evidence. Yet, we believe it is necessary to distinguish them to cut deeper into their characterizing features. In fact, what we call historical-reconstructive pluralism is inextricably tied to the places and dynamics that authors study. Therefore seldom do theories of this type intend to advance a general method for revising contemporary legal and political forms of organization. Rather, their main purpose is to shed light on the nuances and contradictions of a given product of history (a particular political arrangement in the here and the now), in such a way as to remove obstacles and correct malfunctions. Pluralists who mainly (or additionally) carry out conceptual analysis, on the contrary, aim to advance (with many differences among them) a sounder conceptual understanding of the legal phenomenon in order for states to adopt reliable instruments to deal with actual circumstances of plurality.

Italian legal historian Paolo Grossi's theory is one of the most effective examples of historical-reconstructive legal pluralism. He lays bare the artificial nature of modern statehood by a thorough exploration of medieval legal reality. Grossi shows how the Middle Ages reflected an understanding of the innermost nature of law, politics and the relationship between them, which is utterly incompatible with the modern mindset. The gist of Grossi's (2010) argument is that the more and more intrusive shadow of the state, from the fourteenth century, ended up colonizing spheres that used to fall outside its orbit. In particular, over time state agencies came to regulate every sphere of social life and, at the same time, to disown any superior sources of justice.

Grossi underscores how, throughout the Middle Ages, the law was considered to be the historical product of many generations, their relation to the territory and the things that they employed in everyday life. Against this customary and tradition-bound way of understanding law and its fountain, Grossi avers, the modern power-holders managed to impose a theory of legal sources whereby they are the ultimate producers of valid law. In the Middle Ages, he goes on to say, the interactions among individuals were regulated by flexible bodies of rules that might vary case by case according to the needs and interests that they were designed to satisfy. The modern state, on the other hand, established a finite set of valid models of interaction, to the extent that every alternative model should be considered as either illegal or not-legal (that is, juridically null).

Yet, it may be useful to take a closer look at Grossi's reconstruction, for he foregrounds a model of legal pluralism that characterizes an ample section of the Western juridico-political trajectory. Although this model is far away from today's legal and political forms, it offers valuable indications for an alternative reading of contemporary social dynamics.

Grossi shows how the medieval legal order (in particular, the high-medieval one) was by no means considered as an artificial product of an authority, but as an order *inscribed in things*, which people were called upon to read and carefully interpret. The nature of this order was not *potestative*, that is to say, imposed from above, but *organizational*, in that it allowed individuals and groups to give themselves an order, or better, to self-organize and to interact in a stable and cooperative structure. Such a law came *from below*, because it emerged out of the interaction between humans and their environment. On this account, there are two main pillars of the medieval conception of law and politics. First, individuals were not believed to be self-sufficient, as they always needed a stable cooperation with each other. Second, political power was believed to be always incomplete, since it was regarded as parasitic on the order into which it was born – a pre-existing social order that no political ruler would be able to destroy. The genuine condition of the possibility of this state of affairs, Grossi remarks, was the absence of the state.

In this scenario, all law was first and foremost *customary law*. Grossi depicts customs as a woodland path initially cleared by ingenious explorers who took the first steps and were soon followed by other individuals who regarded this path as dependable. To put it otherwise, customary law arises as the habitual reiteration over time of the same conducts by the members of a community (or at least by the bulk of them), to the extent that the conducts in question are adopted as standards of assessment backed up by widespread agreement. The vast range of customs, inevitably bound up with the geo-historical context in which they emerged, is what Grossi calls *medieval constitution*, because it literally *constituted* the community of people who recognized themselves as a community in the light of their shared customs. The legislator, or better, the various legislators existing at the time, did not consider themselves as *makers* of the law, but as *gatherers* and *systematizers* of an impressive set of disjointed laws.

Grossi argues that something changed in the twelfth century upon the revival of the Roman law contained in the *Corpus iuris civilis* – a remarkable summary of Roman juridical knowledge and customs from the origin to the late empire produced under emperor Justinian between 529 and 534. Re-elaborated by a large number of professors of law and legal experts, this impressive stock of legal knowledge was able to provide a new foundation of validity for legal provisions and judicial decisions. Medieval lawyers took Roman law as a point of departure with a view to adapting it to the new circumstance – initially through short glosses alongside the original manuscript and subsequently through extensive comments, which sometimes extensively reinterpreted the letter of the law. The legacy of Roman law then supplemented customs as an additional source of law. Nonetheless, Grossi insists, Roman law did not serve as a stock of abstract precepts and formulae to be applied literally to social reality. This text lent itself to the capacity of skilful legal experts to interpret and adapt a lost tradition to a new reality. In fact, as the generations of lawyers succeeded, the body of glosses and comments grew bigger than the original Roman text, which sometimes turned out to be completely (and often intentionally) misinterpreted and even contradicted.

In this multilayered context, pluralism became even more complex and radical and transmuted into a composite dialectic between the *iura propria* (particular laws) of local communities and a shared body of *ius commune* (common law), that is, a mixture of Roman law and canon law, integrated by sectorial orderings, like the *lex mercatoria*. Common law, Grossi argues, was a creation of jurists attempting to adapt a millennial body of legal knowledge to the changes of times and social conditions. Such a new legal and political scenario was constitutively plural since there were many competing types of law, many competing sources and many competing courts.

This is, in Grossi's view, the acme of legal pluralism and the historical evidence of its richness. We can thus omit Grossi's account of the events that led to the construction of the modern state. A brief sketch will suffice. The momentous transformations that occurred in the fourteenth century brought about a profound revision of the socio-anthropological scenario of European societies: the two pillars of the medieval juridico-political order, mentioned above, were literally overturned. The new social conditions favoured the demise of communitarian values and the advancement of an individualist idea of a self-sufficient human being. At the same time, political power struggled to remove and transcend erstwhile limitations that were designed to tame its innate despotic inclinations. In this new state of affairs, above all in Continental Europe, the law acquired an entirely new shape, as something artificial (that is, created from nothingness and able to shape social reality) produced by an authoritative will (in keeping with the principle that law is law only insofar as it is laid down by a lawmaker).

Such a new conception of law was apposite to the new centripetal claims of sovereigns ('sovereign' was quite an unusual word at the time, as it was forged in the fourteenth century) who had striven to increase their independence from the traditional centres of power (namely, the Church and the Empire) and who aimed to make their autonomy absolute (that is, released from ties, obligations, or constraints upon their activity). Between the fifteenth and the seventeenth centuries many decisive fractures occurred both in terms of actual politics and in terms of political and legal thinking. Social, economic and intellectual forces teamed up in order to favour the ascension of the new sovereign states. These were now conceived as the only legitimate power-holders: producers of valid laws authorized to enforce them with recourse to legitimate violence. The apex of this movement is represented by the diffusion of legal Enlightenment, that Grossi defines as 'legalistic' and even 'legilatrous': in the wake of humanism and natural law theories, a large group of intellectuals, supported by the sovereigns of the most relevant European states, took it upon themselves to promote a new model of state along with a new conception of sovereignty, on which centripetal tendencies of political elites and the needs of the emerging bourgeoisie could converge. This group of intellectuals, comprised of jurists and philosophers, strained to demonstrate that erstwhile pluralism had turned into a chaotic *particularism* that was hindering social development and individual emancipation.

In the middle of the eighteenth century, this wide-ranging project gave way to a copious production of legal codes. Grossi explains how the main goal of the processes of codification and constitutionalization, massively carried out across the Old Continent (with a few exceptions), was to brush away the previous social order and to set up a new one, based on the sacredness of property rights and the inflexible credo in the will of the state. These legal productions brought in the idea that the state is the one and only keeper of a functional, rational order, able to secure certainty and to ward off the vagueness, obscurity and chaos of the medieval legal framework. At the same time, this cultural revolution contributed to spreading the idea that individuals are endowed by birth with a set of rights, and above all the right to property – even though participation rights were still conditional on patrimonial credentials.

The phase of European history inaugurated by the French revolution represents the successful completion of this project. In Grossi's analysis, this phase came to an end with the two World Wars, which exposed the contradictions and flaws of the state paradigm and cleared the way for a new idea of constitution to materialize: contrary to the positivist ideology of the state as a person, the constitution has nothing to do with the will of the lawmaker. Rather, it is the expression and representation of a plural civil society. Grossi (2003) avers that the constitutions of the post-war period stand out as luminous examples of a project, higher and stronger than the capricious whims of the political power-holder in the here and the now, which is enshrined in a chart and needs to be fully accomplished through a common and responsible effort by the civil society as a whole. In this respect, Grossi's view is close to that of neo-constitutional thinkers (see 1.1.3).

The type of pluralism that we defined above as 'historical-reconstructive' focuses on the relationship between the legal systems that

Western states over the past two centuries have exported outside the West and those of the populations who have remained faithful to their traditional orderings in the interstices of everyday life.

In the introduction to a collective book devoted to the relationship between indigenous laws of Asia and transplanted laws, Masaji Chiba (1986) excoriates traditional jurisprudential paradigms that distort and misinterpret what he calls 'received law'. This is neither indigenous law (that is, the law in force before colonial authorities imposed their law) nor transplanted law (that is, the law enforced by colonial authorities). The way the former used to be in the past can no longer be cognized, since it has undergone irreversible changes. Also the latter, however, was altered, in that any transplant presupposes adjustments.

As a first step, Chiba critically canvasses ethnocentric jurisprudential approaches that (whether knowingly or not) apply to non-Western realities a conceptual framework modelled on Western state legal systems. This myopic attitude gradually led to the identification of *Western* law with the law *as such*. Because of this, the history of non-Western societies was erroneously deemed to be the history of the law transplanted in colonial regimes, to the extent that scholars were totally blind to the relevant role played by non-Western law in colonial regimes.

The basic flaw affecting Western-oriented conceptions is that they tend to see the law as a mere system of control in the hands of official agencies and backed up by the threat for non-compliance. At face value, this idea of law may seem to be universally applicable: a legal system can be said to be in force wherever a coercive system of control administered by officials is at work. However, a closer scrutiny proves this view to be ethnocentric, biased, distorting and hence incapable of providing a sound account of a far more complex reality. What is more, this view has too often served the interests of those who wanted to introduce a new (imported) Western-type law to the detriment of the many original orderings. Indeed, while the introduction of a system of control like our modern legal orders blatantly facilitated the takeover of a given society, this was often disguised as a full-hearted commitment to the achievement of peace and the improvement of people's social condition. Such a hypocritical stance produced deleterious outcomes not only (and obviously) on populations but also on political and legal theorizing: the diffusion of a 'legicentric' vision of law and the minimization of the transformative abilities of non-officials in everyday life.

Chiba's analysis does not limit itself to the condemnation of the ethnocentric bias and the imperialistic tendencies of Western law and legal scholarship. He approaches the study of received law as a form of interaction and mutual exchange between indigenous and transplanted laws within a cultural scenario that has remarkably affected the dynamics of this encounter. Frictions and incongruities profoundly affected the way in which native populations managed to preserve and nurture their original laws, in such a way for them to be integrated within the law of dominant populations. This is why, Chiba insists, theorists ought to adopt a historical and culture-specific approach, able to scrutinize and make sense of single events in the light of the broader picture.

If it is true that law is a constituent part of the culture of a population, and that a culture consists of differentiated sets of experiences and fragmented frameworks of knowledge, then the law itself is a plural phenomenon, for it consists of different sets of regulations that are partly coherent and partly conflicting. Chiba claims that in order for theorists to understand this multifarious phenomenon in non-Western countries, they need to deconstruct rigid Western categories like 'legal', 'non-legal' and 'extra-legal', and to do away with the traditional division between 'private' and 'public' law. The conceptual scheme that should guide a study of non-Western law is a tripartite model that allows three levels of legal reality to be distinguished: 'official law', 'unofficial law' and 'legal postulates'.

Official law is the legal system sanctioned by political authorities. State law is a typical expression of official law, as it is directly enforced by the government of a state within its jurisdiction. Yet, in many geo-historical contexts this is not the only source of official law, in that, for example, religious law is an integral part of state law and in some cases it enjoys a high degree of autonomy. Canon law, Islamic law, Hindu law and Hebraic law are typical and well-known instances. But it is often the case that families, professional corporations, social groups and ethnic minorities are subject to separate normative regimes, where dedicated non-state authorities are at work.

Unofficial law signifies a fairly common phenomenon, that is, the numerous sets of regulations supported by the acceptance of all or part of a range of people (this type of acceptance is often tacit and intuitive, as it is inscribed in the routine practices of daily life). These regulations, Chiba explains, have a genuine legal value only insofar as they support, or are at odds with, official law. In fact, it is vital that the latter be in tune with widespread social practices for it to be truly effective and to avoid potential conflicts between official norms and the norms of everyday life (we will return to this issue when discussing conceptual legal pluralism).

Legal postulates are nothing other than a set of ideals, values and principles that give life to the symbolic universe to which the law is party. Legal postulates can be political-legal ideals (such as justice and fairness), sacred truths or religious precepts issued by gods, functional assumptions instrumental in the reproduction of society (such as exogamy, bilinear descent, seniority, individual freedom) or political ideologies connected with economic policies (such as capitalism or socialism). Since they are the basis of the symbolic horizon of an entire population, legal norms have to embody and sanction them, much as they might sometimes be at odds with other features of the legal system.

Chiba's (1989) tripartite model overcomes the traditional opposition between indigenous law and transplanted law to depict received law as the upshot of a more intricate dichotomy. Received law is a dialectic between official law and unofficial law, legal norms and legal postulates, indigenous law and transplanted law. This sophisticated conceptual grid allows going beyond traditional clichés to look at law as an arena where different types of regulation, with different historical backgrounds and different addressees, interact in a dynamic and original way.

Nonetheless, an ambiguity lies at the core of Chiba's analysis of legal pluralism, one that prevents a full assessment of its potential. The notion of culture that underpins Chiba's theorizing when he avers that there is a deep and inextricable tie between a population's cultural background and their law is not clear. At times he seems to hold onto an idea of cultures as distinct and homogeneous monoliths, founded on unquestionable legal postulates. At other times he seems to espouse the image of fragmented collectivities that respond to an equally fragmented, and yet common, body of laws. Moreover, the author fails to clarify whether the phenomenon of legal pluralism stems from the encounter between types of laws (and thus is a mere product of this encounter of cohesive legal orderings) or whether it is an inner characteristic of legal regimes (and thus is an intrinsic trait of every legal ordering).

As a matter of fact, a clearer picture of legal pluralism would show not only the way in which Western law and legal theory have long misinterpreted non-Western realities; it would also cast light on Western legal systems as internally plural and multilayered orders. In other words, a more cogent theory of legal pluralism would be able to deliver a sharp attack on mainstream juristic views on Western politics and law, as it would prove that the legal system of modern national states is inherently plural, like its medieval and early modern predecessors.

This is one of the starting points of *conceptual legal pluralism* – which, needless to say, is never merely conceptual, because it draws on fieldwork research and empirical studies. Most legal pluralists intend to pave the way for an overall revision of existing jurisprudential paradigms, beyond traditional conceptions that see law as a homogeneous entity and state law as the basic prototype of law. Rather, legal pluralists argue, law is a field where distinct normative entities intersect and interact, while state law is nothing but one of the many types of law.

Legal pluralism officially and successfully entered the scene of the international debate in 1978, when the International Union of Anthropological and Ethnological Sciences gave birth to the Commission on Folk Law and Legal Pluralism. This is a working group, still active, that aims to further knowledge and understanding of legal pluralism, with a special focus on theoretical and practical problems resulting from the interaction of different types of law. The Commission on Legal Pluralism is remarkably significant, yet is one of many expressions of a broader movement that gradually got under way in the second half of the twentieth century.

In truth, prominent scholars had already provided insightful accounts of the innate plurality of the legal phenomenon at the beginning of the twentieth century, among them Italian jurist Santi Romano and German legal sociologist Eugen Ehrlich. Despite their different understanding of pluralism, both maintained that there is a compelling case to be made against the idea that law is a fixed system of rules administered and implemented by state officials. On the contrary, Romano and Ehrlich claim, the heart of the legal phenomenon is the self-organizing activity of the various groups of civil society. Families, private clubs, sports clubs, churches, unions, parties and even criminal organizations are characterized by two features that state-centric legal paradigms believe to be the distinguishing mark of state legal systems: first, a given set of rules governing the activity of members and, second, a restricted group of individuals who oversee and administer the application of rules. According to both Ehrlich and Romano, the rules and procedures of these non-official normative contexts guide the conduct of people in a much more effective way than the rules and procedures of state law. Official legal codes would be dead letter unless they relied (whether overtly or covertly) on the non-legal rules of non-state normative regimes and unless they fended off those regimes (like the Mafia) that prove incompatible with the others.

Without a doubt, these minority perspectives seemed quite counter-intuitive in a period when state competencies and powers were growing beyond any expectation. In effect, from the second half of the twentieth century, the cradle of legal pluralism was neither legal theory nor legal sociology (Romano's and Ehrlich's respective fields of study), if only because these disciplines were still engulfed in the ideology of legal centralism. Yet, it was rather the ethno-graphic accounts of non-Western populations (such as, for instance, the Kapauku of Western New Guinea or the Chagga of Mount Kilimanjaro) that gave a new impulse to the study of legal pluralism.

In this regard, a further forerunner of legal pluralism is Polish ethnographer Bronisław Malinowski, active in the first decades of the twentieth century. He contributed significantly to eroding the myth that the phenomenon of law is confined to developed societies and that primitive societies are governed by custom and tradition. In reality, Malinowski can be (improperly) defined as a pluralist mainly on account of the influential notion of law he put forward. This notion lies at the heart of many legal-pluralist proposals because it provides a non-conventional portrayal of the legal phenomenon that extends to that which mainstream theorists straightforwardly regarded as social normativity. Malinowski viewed law as a particular set of rules felt and regarded as the obligations of one person and the rightful claims of another. These rules are sanctioned by a well-defined social machinery of binding force, based on mutual dependence and reciprocity. On this reading, the core of the legal phenomenon rests on a sophisticated social mechanism that fosters mutual cooperation and makes sure that non-compliant people get punished.

In brief, the pillars of legal pluralism are three. First, law is a form of organization based upon rules and institutionalized procedures, which constitute the core structure of a given population (this term broadly referring to a set of people, no matter how many, subject to the same set of rules) or the same field of interaction (sport, trade, religion, etc.). Secondly, as an organizational structure, law is what ensures the stable reproduction of this population (regardless of their technical and technological development) or this field (regardless of its inner complexity). Thirdly, if the first two assumptions hold, then the corollary is that in a given geo-historical context there are as many legal orders as the populations and fields at work within it. Based on this picture, legal pluralism can be regarded as an inescapable trait of human sociality.

From within the Western tradition, John Griffiths's (1986) article 'What is Legal Pluralism?' capitalizes on the contributions mentioned above and other sources to debunk the idea that legal systems are homogeneous entities and that a clear-cut line can be drawn between legal and non-legal phenomena. To this end, Griffiths bridges anthropological findings on non-Western populations and sociological analyses of Western states to redraw the borders of the concept of law in the West. He claims that in Western states the plurality of legal forms is not an element from a remote past, but affects present-day societies. In doing so, he nicely delineates the polemic target of most legal pluralists, that is, legal centralism. This is a view that, according to Griffiths, depicts law as a product of the state, uniform for all people, exclusive of all other law and administered by a single set of state institutions; at the same time, all other social orderings present in society (churches, universities, unions, private organizations, political parties, trade companies) are considered to be hierarchically subordinate to the state law and state institutions.

If legal centralism can be said to be the common enemy of most pluralists, it is yet much harder to offer a general definition of legal pluralism. Griffiths speaks of it as a circumstance, typical of every social field, where individual conducts are subject to more than one ordering. In reality, he is describing a rather familiar and widespread phenomenon: we can imagine a girl who as a daughter obeys household rules, as a student the rules of her university, as a football player the rules of football, while at the same time she is (whether consciously or not) to a greater or lesser extent affected by a series of regulations that govern her conduct as a friend, a partner, an employee, a client, a consumer and so on. Griffiths's claim is that seeing all these sets of rules as non-legal, and thus as outside the field of law, is a serious theoretical mistake, in that they govern the life of subjects much more effectively than state rules. In fact, every social field – a notion that he takes from legal anthropologist Sally Falk Moore (2000) – has its own inner order, comprised of a set of rules that, on the one hand, distinguishes this field from others and, on the other hand, turns an aggregate of individuals into an organized collectivity. Society is nothing other than an ensemble of semi-autonomous social fields (though not entirely autonomous, as they always interact and influence each other). Griffiths's conclusion is that state law is only one order among many others: it has its own rules and its range of addressees (which most often correspond to the whole constituency of a given country), but should acknowledge the existence of other fields, governed by other orders. This view, Griffiths insists, is not *normative*, since it does not aim to offer guidelines on the reform of contemporary states. Rather, he claims it is *descriptive* and simply provides the right angle to observe juridico-political dynamics.

However, Griffiths's hyperextension of the concept of law gives rise to a basic aporia: the state is an order among others and yet it manages to overrule them. In the end, he fails to bring out the difference (whether it is normative, ontological, historical or merely ideological) between the law and the other social orders. To spell this out, and to offer a stronger account of legal pluralism, it is worth examining two sophisticated – but not entirely reconcilable – theories: Franz von Benda-Beckmann's and Gordon R. Woodman's.

We would like to note that the analysis of legal pluralism offered by these authors is highly instructive insofar as they make some relevant points about the central issue of this book, that is, how different theoretical approaches account for the changes that are affecting contemporary states. As in the case of multiculturalism, legal pluralism runs the risk of providing a rigid, objectifying and reifying notion of groups, as if these were homogeneous and autonomous entities, able to structure their internal life irrespective of other subjects or entities living in the same social space. Were this objectifying view to be true, the heart of law would be the inner order of the discrete groups, that is, the norms and procedures that make a given group that group. However, this tantalizing association between the idea of groups as totalities and the view of law as the groups' inner normative framework leads to the aporia described above. Quite the contrary, the authors taken into exam here deploy a conception of law as a highly flexible phenomenon. Scholars and researchers, von Benda-Beckmann and Woodman contend, are seldom (if ever) confronted with homogeneous totalities. Fieldwork and observation concern nested and overlapping normative entities within societies that are often (if not always) highly fragmented. As we will show, this idea of legal order is characterized by a high degree of flexibility and indeterminacy.

Benda-Beckmann (2002) sees legal pluralism as an analytical tool that is meant to help scholars ascertain similarity and difference in cross-societal and diachronic comparison. In stark contrast with Griffiths's account, legal pluralism is not the description of a state of affairs that is already and always plural, but the defence of the *theoretical possibility* (to be proven with recourse to empirical evidence) that the models elaborated at a conceptual level actually coexist in the same time and space. While this seems to narrow the scope of pluralism as a social phenomenon (since it is no longer seen as an inescapable condition of social life), Benda-Beckmann unravels the 'panlegalist' aporia that sees every form of social coexistence as *ipso facto* being *legal*. Indeed, in one way or another, Ehrlich, Romano and Griffiths come to the conclusion that every social group or field of interaction is to be regarded as having a genuinely legal order that is as valid and legitimate as the law of the state. Benda-Beckmann shows that not every small aggregate of individuals, albeit organized, amounts to a legal entity. Rather, it is the theorist's duty to determine what distinctive characteristics social phenomena must possess in order for them to be meaningfully considered as 'legal'.

On the other hand, the analytical toolkit should be broad enough to accommodate a wide set of phenomena: it is little use approaching legal reality with a predetermined definition in mind, no matter whether it is inspired by a centralistic or a pluralistic view. The conceptual map has to make room for all these possibilities and many others. In other words, Benda-Beckmann insists, theorists have to do away with any conceptual prejudice that could distort, misconstrue or misread the subject of study.

Against any reductionism, Benda-Beckmann claims that even though law most often takes the shape of a set of binding prescriptions, it is mainly a set of *cognitive* indications involved in the construction of social reality. Legal fact-types (such as property, sale, rental, marriage and testament) establish what counts as a valid action and/or interaction in a given geo-historical context and, at the same time, exclude alternative actions and/or interactions. The types of actions and interactions whose validity has been legally established are presented as binding and, when necessary, backed up by sanction, while the others are considered as null from a legal vantage point and thus devoid of official consequences (two individuals may regard themselves as spouses in their private life, but cannot enjoy the privileges connected to this status unless they are given the seal of official recognition). In doing so, the law promotes a series of 'objectified reifications' (at both a public level, such as citizenship or representation, and at a private one, such as contract or property), with which rule-abiders are required to conform if they want their actions to have legal consequences.

If this is so, then not every human collectivity can count on such a framework of knowledge and rules. Benda-Beckmann concludes that, in order to be defined as legal, a given social phenomenon must be assessed according to specific, although changing, variables: the scope of institutionalization; the extent to which knowledge, interpretation and application of law have been differentiated from everyday knowledge; the extent of professionalization, theorization and scientification; the extent to which legal rules are defined as mandatory; the technology of transmission; the social and/or geographical scope for which validity is asserted; the type of foundation that gives it validity (be it a customary practice, a social contract or a written constitution).

On this reading, legal pluralism is *the inquiry into the variables whereby something can be regarded as law.* Pluralism in the legal field consists in the synchronic occurrence of differentiated processes. Coexistence is not regarded as the simultaneous presence of bordered groups with their own inner orders, but as *a continuous and multi-level exchange among diversified sets of knowledge and rules,* more or less institutionalized, more or less professionalized, more or less extensive. The view underlying strong multiculturalism is thus reversed: political reform should not pursue the enhancement of non-state autonomous jurisdictions, but the extension of the traditional conception of law with a view to accommodating new processes, fact-types and procedures, and to widening the scope and extension of the legal system.

Law is no longer seen as a set of rules supported by force but as an irregular and nested ensemble of knowledge and rules: Benda-Beckmann (2002) mentions several examples (above all non-Western ones) where the process of state recognition of religious and indigenous law leads to many productive exchanges, which affect each of them and help them accommodate social change.

Woodman (2009) reaches rather different conclusions. On the one hand, he reinforces and even radicalizes pluralism, as he goes so far as to deny that Western law has nothing truly distinctive. On the other hand, based on that, he claims that at a theoretical level little can be said about the coexistence of types of laws, in that only empirical investigations can provide reliable results.

Woodman foregrounds the conditions that determine states of pluralisms by analysing the nature of the type of law usually defined as 'customary' (which is quite a controversial notion, in that some authors think that this type really constitutes a genuine form of indigenous law practised by colonized populations, while others deem it to be an artificial product brought to life by the encounter between natives and colonials). Customary law is depicted as a set of rules that prescribe or prohibit conducts, confer powers, specify the legal consequences that follow from voluntary forms of conduct, specify the legal consequences of natural events (such as the rules of succession on death), and define concepts (such as 'family' or 'father'). The rules of this type of law derive their validity and content from acceptance and observance on the part of a given populations (again: this term should be understood broadly, as a range of individuals, no matter how many, subject to the same set of rules). Within this form of law, rules are not seen as imperatives issued by a legislative agency, but serve as public standards of conduct that allow people both to assess the behaviour of each other (and thus to criticize what rules establish as incorrect) and to engage in interactions recognized as valid.

Building on this analysis, Woodman's argument takes a twofold path. On the one hand, he claims that this type of law captures the essence of the legal phenomenon. On the other hand, he demonstrates that the definition mentioned above, from a descriptive point of view, adequately captures not only the type of law we are most familiar with, but every set of rules governing the social life of sub-state and generally sectorial populations (ethnic groups, professional and labour associations, prison inmate groups, slave classes or a class of conscripted soldiers).

Following the first path, Woodman criticizes the common mistaken assumption that customary law is a spurious type of law, since it is believed to lack some typical traits of legislative law. He rebuts this tenet by showing that customary law possesses all essential traits of legislative law. Precisely like the latter, customary law frequently contains procedures for law-making which amount to legislation. Yet, the most robust claim levelled by Woodman is that state law is based on a custom, whereby official agencies authorized to create and enforce laws follow the same meta-rule (which can be set in a written constitution or can take the shape of an unstated but consolidated practice). Therefore, state law is nothing but a particular type of customary law, the populations that observe it being the officials and others who operate in the various institutions of the state.

Following the second path, Woodman shows that, given that 'state law' is a species of the genus 'customary law' and given that any set of public standards of conduct governing the inner dynamics of a population also belongs to this genus, no clear distinction can be drawn between the multiple forms of regulation that arise in human social life and the particular set of rules that people call 'law' in the here and the now. In other words, Woodman argues that there is no clear distinctive line between legal and non-legal rules.

If this is true, then the primacy of a type of law over the others cannot be justified from a conceptual standpoint, but, as it were, is based on a relation of power: the law of one population (those that operate in the various institutions of the state) acquires a higher position and demotes the laws of other populations. To make up for such an iniquitous condition, it has to be understood and reframed in terms of coexistence of equally legitimate legal orders and has to be overcome by means of recognition.

First of all, Woodman singles out four conditions of legal pluralism in which the state may be involved, while the policies that may be adopted by the state towards a non-state law may be regarded as different possible relations between the two laws. These conditions are: *concurrence*, when the norms of the two laws require identical behaviour; *conflict*, when the norms of the two laws contradict each other; *agglomeration*, when without a planned relationship between the norms of the two laws, they refer to different activities, so that they neither contradict nor influence each other; and *integration*, when there is a planned relationship between the norms of the two laws, so that by design they refer to different activities and avoid conflict.

Woodman explains that contemporary states tend to favour integration because it does not seek to suppress the other law by norms that conflict with it. This type of condition, however, can take two different shapes: *self-determination for the non-state law population* or *recognition*.

These are quite different models. Self-determination entails a self-limitation by the state of its own jurisdiction. The state defines a field of activity over which it will not exercise jurisdiction, which is left to the control of the institutions and rules of the non-state law. The state accepts that a greater or lesser degree of independence will be exercised by the non-state law population. Recognition can be of two types: *normative recognition* (when state agencies take it upon themselves to give effect to the norms of another law), and *institutional recognition* (when state law incorporates the institutions of another law within its own institutional structure). In political terms, recognition may be said to be the demonstration of respect for the other law or for the population that observes it.

Woodman suggests that a promising candidate in the accommodation of pluralism is normative recognition, whereby the various types of non-state customary laws can be adequately reformulated in order for them to integrate with the normative and institutional system that gives recognition. The state in its turn can promote internal reforms to make room for the rules and institutions of the non-state law. However, Woodman continues, the recognition of a set of norms is always a creative process. Even with an adequate understanding of a customary law, recognition involves reformulation that has to be made deliberately and with a skill informed by knowledge of other comparable instances.

For present purposes, it may be said that both versions of legal pluralism examined thus far seem to overcome the impasse that affects multiculturalism: even though Benda-Beckmann and Woodman place emphasis (even more radically than multicultural theorists) on the need to go over state legal monism, both appear to reach the conclusion that the creation of autonomous jurisdictions may favour a pathological seclusion of groups. Quite the reverse, what political institutions need to do is set up a platform for exchange and interaction where responsibilities are split equally between state and non-state parties. In this framework, law can serve as a complex field of transformative negotiation and mediation, where the various forms of regulations are called upon to integrate with one another.

3.2 The law, the market and the demise of politics

3.2.1 Juridification or de-politicization?

The theories analysed in the previous section insist on the obsolescence of the idea of the sole legislator, represented by state government, and espouse a concept of law as a form of self-organization typical of a variety of social entities, whether small or big. Nonetheless, the relationship with the state as an indispensable actor in the process of negotiation is believed to be essential: if, from a theoretical viewpoint, state legal systems are nothing other than orders among others, from a pragmatic viewpoint they maintain the monopoly on power in most areas of the world. Against this persistent centrality of the state, some authors, whether or not committed to a pluralist view, put much more stress on the processes of legislative production that fall outside the orbit of the state. These processes, they claim, are genuine building blocks of a global juridico-political order that will end up transcending the state once and for all. In this reading, the buzzwords are (stateless) 'juridification' and 'constitutionalization', that is, a set of processes through which some societal sectors produce rules of their own independently of traditional legal procedures.

Günther Teubner (1991) speaks of legal pluralism as a multiplicity of communicative processes that subsume the activities of social actors under the binary code 'legal/illegal'. All the types of interactions that, whether explicitly or implicitly, adopt this code as a common system of reference *ipso facto* migrate into the legal field and thus contribute to fuelling the phenomenon of society's spontaneous juridification (that is, a production of rules considered as neither conventional nor moral, but instrumental in the definition of what is legal and what is not legal in a given sector).

Such sectors lay bare the demise of the state and bring into question its monopoly over legitimacy. In other words, any social sector can adopt the binary code legal/illegal and, in so doing, juridifies itself, even when a sector is considered as illegal by the state legal system. A criminal gang, for example, whether or not its members are formally outlaws, constitutes an autonomous sphere, where the binary code legal/illegal is applied in an idiosyncratic but functional manner.

This is why, in Teubner's view, the relation between the state and indigenous laws does not exhaust the question of legal pluralism. Rather this should help describe the increasing fragmentation of society as the production of a multiplicity of legally autonomous discourses. Teubner (2004) then addresses the new phenomenon of global juridification as a shift towards *societal constitutionalism* consisting in the emergence of a multiplicity of civil constitutions, that is, the constitutionalization of a multiplicity of autonomous sub-systems of the world society. This is a process that is taking place at the peripheries of law and withdraws the traditional centres of law-making (such as national parliaments, global legislative institutions and intergovernmental agreements). Teubner clarifies that this process does not only involve juridification. It is not all about the mere creation of legal rules of conduct valid in a certain sector. Rather, constitutionalization is first and foremost instrumental in the creation of this very sector. To put it differently, autonomous rule production is crucial to the formation of sectorial constitutions. Societal sectors determine their own criteria of self-reproduction, set the standards by which to discriminate between valid and invalid norms and establish specific agencies that oversee such processes.

It is worth noting that the notion of societal constitutionalism developed by Teubner breaks with the traditional image of constitution as a phase of coalescence of politics and law. A constitution is regarded as an instrument of self-production, autonomously employed within a given societal sector. He traces and describes such genetic mutations brought about by the inner turmoil of a decentred global society that is tearing apart the classical constitutional frame of fully fledged and late modernity. Trapped in the functional logics of a global society, the constitution disposes of its political traits and migrates into the extra-state legal field, wherein the goal is not to create objectives shared by all social parties and to grant them equal opportunities, but to draw the boundaries of the self-constitution-alizing sector and to set standards of internal administration that ensure its stability and reproduction.

An exemplar case is the forceful emergence of a type of non-state regulation of private interaction in the trade network, known as '*lex mercatoria*'. Born in the low Middle Ages as a 'caste-law' instru-mental in the production of common and non-territorial rules for merchants, contemporary *lex mercatoria* (Ferrarese 2006) challenges the normative primacy of domestic legal orders: it turns the image of the state as the source radiating legal norms into a passive receiver of inputs produced by economic bodies creating rules of their own. In effect, financial organizations prospering in the trade network provide themselves with autonomous mechanisms of rule-making (quite different from legislative institutions of traditional states) and rule-applying (quite different from traditional courts), which allow a self-government outside the sphere of state politics. According to Maria Rosaria Ferrarese, such a stateless and society-centred law is regaining some key features of medieval law. On the one hand, modern *lex mercatoria* gets its validity out of its customary nature, in that only constant reiteration confers legal validity on a given normative standard; on the other hand, in order for the outcomes of customary practices to turn into binding and general standards, they undergo a process of elaboration on the part of specialists (lawyers, consultants, experts in trade law). In this reading, contemporary *lex mercatoria* is not a general law comprised of imperatives, but a custom practised by a multiplicity of actors that acquires a normative character by virtue of an elaborative process carried out by learned experts. The customary and juristic nature of *lex mercatoria* is eroding the grammar of modern state laws (above all the civil law tradition) and emerges as a new laboratory for a transnational stateless law.

The chaos brought about by the growing constitutional pluralism, according to Ferrarese, should urge political and legal theorists to replace the concept of 'border' (inextricably tied to the history of the state) with that of 'frontier'. Whereas the former excludes and always cuts someone out, the latter more modestly draws the line of a horizon that is never set in stone. This view that removes fixities and highlights uncertainties proposes suspending judgement over contemporary transitions and assessing advantages and ambivalences step by step. Indeed, it is not always the case that circumstantial legal productions and the break with traditional normative hierarchies have positive effects. More specifically, the connection between legal rationality and market logics may turn out to promote the cause of certain types of individual rights meant to protect private liberties and entrepreneurial freedom at the expense of more 'expensive' rights, such as social ones, requiring significant investments that might be at odds with the former type of rights (Catania 2008).

Despite these opacities, there are those who are confident that the transitions discussed so far are for the better. Authors such as Paul Schiff Berman and Nico Krisch have developed a theoretical model, known as 'global legal pluralism', which aspires to capture at best these transitions so as to demonstrate how the latter introduce elements of fruitful plurality and workable conflict. Berman (2012) insists that the ideas of an ultimate legal authority (whether national or international) and of state sovereignty have to be jettisoned. Global law and the proliferation of legal sites at the supranational level pave the way for a new juridico-political scenario, one that is based on relationships and exchanges among multiple communities and their decision makers. According to Berman, this condition of legal hybridity is first and foremost a *de facto* reality, which is, however, *normatively* virtuous, because normative conflicts among multiple, overlapping legal systems can be a source of alternative ideas and a site for discourse among multiple community affiliations.

In short, there are two main virtues of this new juridico-political scenario. The first, epistemic virtue has to do with the recognition of a multiplicity of legal sources beyond the state which calls for more respect for social groups as autonomous creators of law. The second, pragmatic virtue is that, in Berman's view, pluralism makes room for contestation and creative adaptation. Pluralism, however, must be regulated through normative proceduralism, since no agreement on the content of substantive principles is possible. In this reading, global legal pluralism is a tool for managing legal hybridity via procedures that give voice to, and empower, different communities. Berman believes that this approach is likely to tame conflict among staunchly different and potentially opposite views of different legal orders. This trait of global legal pluralism, in many respects, seems to be rooted in a liberal political perspective, especially in that it postulates that voices have a right to be heard insofar as they are capable of advancing *reasonable* arguments.

Krisch (2011) starts off from what he views as a bare fact, which is that different layers of law in the postnational order no longer operate in separate spheres but are deeply intertwined. In his perspective, pluralism is not only a prism that allows a better understanding of the structure of law; pluralism is also a normative, even radical standpoint. There are three main virtues in the new global scenario: revisability, checks and balances, and contestation. If revisability means that there is no ultimate authority, while checks and balances are made available through the very proliferation of sites of authority, only contestation makes up for the lack of trust that is currently engendered by the absence of a direct connection between social actors and supranational institutions. Contestation is made possible by the fact that interactions at the supranational level are regulated by 'interface norms' which signal enmeshment and joint engagement in a common space. For courts, for example, this would mean disposing of a self-perception as the guardians of their own legal orders and embracing the role of mediators or arbiters among orders, in that they themselves would be the bearers of many legal identities at one and the same time.

Yet, there are less optimistic views on these transitions, views that perceive various elements of ambiguity in the hybridity and fuzziness of the global juridico-political scenario. Within this critical view, the spate of rules and procedures produced at the supra-state level is regarded as an effect of a new complex, 'neo-liberal' model of government. Wendy Brown (2005) forcefully claims that what is now called 'neo-liberalism' is a rationality, in contrast to those analyses that view neo-liberalism as a bundle of economic policies with inadvertent political and social consequences. She insists that the novelty of this form of rationality is inscribed in the prefix 'neo': it stands for something radically new, which indicates a deep rupture with traditional liberal and conservative approaches. The latter aimed to deprive the state of its onerous task of redistributing wealth and opportunities, tied to what right-wing liberals and conservatives deemed to be an obese, overabundant, corporative welfare state. Quite the reverse, neo-liberalism emerges as a 'constructivist' project, with a powerfully normative, or better, disciplinary inclination, which is meant not so much to cut, slim, put on a diet, but to transform and mould (Dardot and Laval 2014). The constructivist force of neo-liberalism turns into a multiple array of discourses and practices instrumental in the *production* of new political subjectivities (one of the epitomes of this project of subjectification is the transformation of citizens into consumers) and to impose a rigid series of criteria to assess things that are inspired by the unquestionable dogma of economic rationality.

In this regard, as Brown points out and as also Antoine Garapon (2010) insists, both of them building on Michel Foucault's analysis in *The Birth of Biopolitics*, neo-liberalism rejects the anthropological myth of enlightened individuals who spontaneously give birth to a system of exchanges orchestrated by innate rules. Neo-liberalism is convinced that the market is not something natural, spontaneous, driven by the magic force of an enlightened self-interest. It must be created artificially. This is the biggest rupture signified by the prefix 'neo': the market, which is portrayed as *the* perfect model of integration, is to be constructed. To this end, any form of regulation that proves not to be compatible with neo-liberalism has to be wiped out and replaced with new compatible forms. This is why neo-liberalism rests on pervasive modes of political intervention in the social realm. In this sense, it endorses a radically artificial and demiurgic view of society: there is a desperate need to provide the conditions for the development of something that must be implanted and promoted with appropriate and effective utensils.

From this point of view, it is possible to appreciate a relevant difference between the classical model of sovereignty and the neo-liberal rationality, that is to say, the *chameleonic compatibility* that makes neo-liberalism a much more effective vehicle of social adjustment with no need to produce relevant, or at least visible, social rifts. Modern sovereignty relied on a potestative, imperative, top-down approach. Modern sovereigns had to invest a lot of money and devote a lot of effort to knocking down the traditional pre-modern system of the *Ancien Régime*. Modern sovereigns reinvented society in all respects: cultural, economic, religious, legal, political and so on. Modern sovereigns had to present themselves as the sole available option in order for their society to survive and blossom, and to do that they needed to take over in every field. Neo-liberalism adopts an entirely different model of action. According to the neo-liberal perspective, the model of sovereignty needs to be discarded once and for all since it is expensive and ineffective in the long run. In the neo-liberal canon, the state needs to concentrate less and less on the coercive regulation of external behaviours and more and more on the production of subjectivities that may prove to be fully compatible with its new model of regulation. This is the reason why Brown maintains that privatization and the resulting withdrawal of the state from many spheres that once it claimed to regulate (such as security and welfare) does not amount to a dismantling of government but rather constitutes a technique of governing. As a 'theory of every-thing', neo-liberalism has and pursues a project of society, which the state (as a set of technical bodies and actual goal-oriented policies) is called upon to accomplish by implementing a law that is pervasive, flexible and able to penetrate: neo-liberal law aims at producing and fostering a yardstick that can be well adapted to any circumstances and contexts, that is to say, the calculable efficiency of the market, which aims to serve as a universal operator.

This also makes sense of the strategic use neo-liberalism makes of the state and its policies. The state can no longer represent the ultimate horizon of a political community that provides itself with a system of self-organization. The state must not exceed its limits, which are set by its own value of means. The state has to see to it that new spaces may be opened up for the thorough diffusion of more effective ways to govern interactions, such as, again, the market and its competitive logic. In so doing, neo-liberalism carries out a homogenizing activity, because the market rationality, as Brown writes, knows no culture or country and administrators are, as the economists say, fungible. Neo-liberalism easily crosses borders by virtue of its inner logic, which can be easily applied to any context or situation, with no further need for a justification based on the history or the culture of the context or situation where it is being applied. But precisely such an easing of the burden of justification and self-legitimation covers up neo-liberalism's ability to penetrate. It offers its own canons as yardsticks that do not require troublesome adjustments, but – and, as we said before, this is a crucial feature of neo-liberalism – operate in a regime of compatibility: all can be squared with it, providing that all can be measured with the yardstick of market rationality. The neo-liberal canon infiltrates by virtue of its unusual mimetism, which enables it to readjust and reshape while latching onto diverse normative regimes: the neo-liberal canon does not conflict with other normative regimes, but slightly changes the lexicon, the functions, the orientation to reality and the semantic spectrum of the rules of these regimes. The inner constructivist force of neo-liberalism is accompanied by an extraordinary transformative one, since it transforms by integrating from outside: neo-liberalism offers itself as a toolkit that can be used spontaneously, without any pressure, in the light of their innate (alleged) efficiency.

3.2.2 Cultural identities *vis-à-vis* the market

Political inquiry as the study of new forms of subjectivities and institutional arrangements is intrinsically related to the anthropological analysis of contemporary forms of life. The latter approach is all the more needed in disquieting times of 'monstrous chimeras', as Jean and John Comaroff (2001) epitomize them. The conflation between the strange and the familiar ignites a change of both the social world and the way people perceive it: legalism and libertarianism, constitutionalism and deregulation, rationalist secularism and esoteric allure join. In this picture, contradictions become the leitmotiv of a type of politics in which everything becomes equally possible. According to the Comaroffs, the peculiar mixture of contradictory elements across the world is due to the new structural product of neo-liberal capitalism, which is pursuing a programme of a global homologation of political structures through a multiplicity of processes: the transfer of political power from state agencies to the global market players, the weakening of public administration, the recourse to a universalizing legal language that overshadows cultural and political differences, the diffusion of new technologies that homologate languages and habits, the transformation of human beings into labour units, commodities and/or clients. In brief, the production of a society controlled and oriented by the law of the market, which endows human beings with a freedom that is as fictitious as it is pervasive in its disruptive effects.

If many authors concur on the analysis of the global neo-liberal shift, what the Comaroffs (2009) describe as the three main effects of it are of particular interest. They speak, first, of an 'incorporation' of identity politics that renders cultures into corporations; secondly, of a 'commodification' of culture when the process of incorporation confers socio-political visibility on identity groups; and thirdly, of a 'fetishization' of law, whereby the transnational and universal character of law prevails over convoluted local policies.

While in the Global North national politics represents a field of battle among enclaves who claim autonomy, in the Global South identity politics takes the path of a 'negotiated commodification', above all in territories where minority cultures have traditionally represented an obstacle to the creation of colonial states. The reviviscence of ancestral traditions, lived and managed as a commodity to trade, is exploited by neglected minorities as a way to acquire visibility, despite the fact that these traditions get completely altered. The Comaroffs illustrate how the renaissance of folklore, which may seem to be rooted in an earnest commitment to political autonomy, shows the mark of misrecognition: much as it brings these minorities into light, folklore is nothing but a parody. This is the case, for example, of Xavante traditional dancers from the Amazon or the Li population of Hainan Island (China): the commodification of their traditional habits and customs often turns out to be crucial to their survival and sustainability. Colourful dances – once meaningful vehicles of sense – are reinvented in unexpected forms and sold to curious tourists. In the market of politics, this grants these populations contractual power, in the quality of authentic ethnic groups that attract curious interest.

Yet, the Comaroffs aver, authenticity is not a stable property of an object or a state of things, but an attribute subject to negotiation, whereby exotic ways of life are tamed and altered. Self-affirmation entails self-overturning, which at once pushes exotic populations into the limelight: the power to have a say in the political arena is directly proportional to the ability to attract an audience in the broad stage of global tourism. This possibility of using traditions as bargaining counters turns identity claims into weapons whose use accords with a market logic.

The marriage of politics and market negotiation favours the rise of law as a new fetish of global politics. John and Jean Comaroff analyse how, in the wake of global politics, law comes to be regarded as a set of standardized symbols and practices that, like money in the sphere of consumption, allow the negotiation of values and interests. Law becomes a universal code in whose light all languages prove to be inter-translatable and all experiences comparable. This view of law sanctifies the triumph of a disfigured and heterodox constitution-alism, which celebrates the simultaneous triumph of individual rights in the hands of international courts of justice, which use the former as pervasive instruments of authority.

The three phenomena discussed so far, according to the Comaroffs, join together and take the shape of a triangle that symbolizes present-day political conditions: while society undergoes changes in the fields of politics, morality and economy, new, artificial forms of ethnic and religious integralism (whether individual or collective) arise and bring into question traditional types of subjectivity, citizenship and collective self-consciousness. The looming shadow of the market transforms politics into a field of commodified and disfigured struggles over identity; at the same time it delegates administrative tasks to the law, whose inner grammar is undergoing an uncritical 'uniformation' (always modelled on the Western experience and with a resolute subjectivist proclivity). A vicious circle – engendered by the proliferation of transversal types of identities, most often religiously connoted – fuels disorder and instability, erodes the public and participatory nature of politics and favours massive recourse to the legal language as a neutral language that allows people to settle social conflicts. Yet, the Comaroffs warn that it would be highly mistaken to see all this as the mere consequence of the rise of a mercantile capitalist rationality. In reality, these processes stem from the deep essence of neo-liberalism and its ability to infiltrate every geo-historical context. Neo-liberalism is nothing but the mystical and self-nurturing conjunction of three elements: the apotheosis of intellectual property and the reduction of culture to a private good of individuals and groups; the dislocation of politics into the field of law (which is presented as) able to produce and validate itself; the transformation of the subject into a self-entrepreneur called upon to make profit out of her own *human capital*.

References

Agamben, Giorgio (1998). *Homo Sacer: Sovereign Power and Bare Life*. Translated by Daniel Heller-Roazen. Stanford, CA: Stanford University Press.

Alexy, Robert (2002). *The Argument from Injustice: A Reply to Legal Positivism*. Translated by Bonnie Litschewski Paulson and Stanley L. Paulson. Oxford: Oxford University Press.

Anderson, Benedict (2006). *Imagined Communities: Reflections on the Origin and Spread of Nationalism*. London and New York: Verso.

Archibugi, Daniele (2008). *The Global Commonwealth of Citizens: Toward Cosmopolitan Democracy*. Princeton, NJ: Princeton University Press.

Avant, Deborah D. (2005). *The Market for Force: The Consequences of Privatizing Security*. Cambridge: Cambridge University Press.

Backford, Jim (2012). 'Public Religions and the Postsecular: Critical Reflections'. *Journal for the Scientific Study of Religion* 51: 1–19.

Bass, Gary Jonathan (2002). *Stay the Hand of Vengeance: The Politics of War Crimes Tribunals*. Princeton, NJ: Princeton University Press.

Bauböck, Rainer (1994). *Transnational Citizenship: Membership and Rights in International Migration*. Aldershot: Elgar.

Bauman, Zygmunt (1999). *In Search of Politics*. Stanford, CA: Stanford University Press.

—(2001). *The Individualized Society*. Cambridge: Polity Press.

Bazzicalupo, Laura (2010). *Biopolitica. Una mappa concettuale*. Roma: Carocci.

Beck, Ulrich (2006). *The Cosmopolitan Vision*. Translated by Ciaran Cronin. Cambridge: Polity Press.

—(2009). *World at Risk*. Translated by Ciaran Cronin. Cambridge: Polity Press.

Bellamy, Richard (2007). *Political Constitutionalism: A Republican Defence of the Constitutionality of Democracy*. Cambridge: Cambridge University Press.

Benda-Beckmann, Franz von (2002). 'Who is Afraid of Legal Pluralism?' *Journal of Legal Pluralism* 47: 37–83.

Benhabib, Seyla (2002). *The Claims of Culture: Equality and Diversity in the Global Era*. Princeton, NJ: Princeton University Press.

Berman, Paul Schiff (2012). *Global Legal Pluralism: A Jurisprudence of Law Beyond Borders*. Cambridge: Cambridge University Press.

Böckenförde, Ernst-Wolfgang (1991). *State, Society, and Liberty: Studies in Political Theory and Constitutional Law*. Translated by J. A. Underwood. New York: Berg.

Brock, Gillian and Brighouse, Harry (2005). *The Political Philosophy of Cosmopolitanism*. Cambridge: Cambridge University Press.

Brown, Garrett W. (2009). *Grounding Cosmopolitanism: From Kant to the Idea of a Cosmopolitan Constitution*. Edinburgh: Edinburgh University Press.

Brown, Wendy (2005). *Edgework: Critical Essays on Knowledge and Politics*. Princeton, NJ: Princeton University Press.

Bull, Hedley (2002). *The Anarchical Society: A Study of Order in World Politics*. New York: Columbia University Press.

Butler, Judith, Laclau, Ernesto and Žižek, Slavoj (2000). *Contingency, Hegemony, Universality: Contemporary Dialogues on the Left*. London: Verso.

Buzan, Barry (1991). *People, States, and Fear: An Agenda for International Security Studies in the Post-Cold War Era*. New York: Harvester Wheatsheaf.

Buzan, Barry and Little, Richard (2000). *International Systems in World History: Remaking the Study of International Relations*. Oxford: Oxford University Press.

Caney, Simon (2005). *Justice Beyond Borders: A Global Political Theory*. Oxford: Oxford University Press.

Caputo, John D. (2001). *On Religion*. London: Routledge.

Casanova, José (1994). *Public Religions in the Modern World*. Chicago: University of Chicago Press.

Catania, Alfonso (2008). *Metamorfosi del diritto. Decisione e norma nell'età globale*. Roma and Bari: Laterza.

Chiba, Masaji (ed.) (1986). *Asian Indigenous Law: In Interaction with Received Law*. London and New York: KPI.

—(1989). *Legal Pluralism: Towards a General Theory Through Japanese Legal Culture*. Tokyo: Tokai University Press.

Colombo, Alessandro (2006). *La guerra ineguale. Pace e violenza nel tramonto della società internazionale*. Bologna: il Mulino.

Comaroff, Jean and Comaroff, John L. (2001). *Millennial Capitalism and the Culture of Neo-liberalism*. Durham: Duke University Press.

—(2009). *Ethnicity, Inc.* Chicago: The University of Chicago Press.

Cover, Robert (1983). 'The Supreme Court 1982 Term, Forward: *Nomos* and Narrative'. *Harvard Law Review* 97: 4–68.

Crouch, Colin (2004). *Post-Democracy*. Cambridge: Polity Press.

—(2011). *The Strange Non-Death of Neoliberalism*. Cambridge: Polity Press.

Dagger, Richard (1997). *Civic Virtues: Rights, Citizenship, and Republican Liberalism*. Oxford: Oxford University Press.

Dardot, Pierre and Laval, Christian (2014). *The New Way of the World: On Neoliberal Society*. Translated by Gregory Elliott. London: Verso.

de Vries, Hent and Sullivan, Lawrence E. (eds) (2006). *Political Theologies: Public Religions in a Post-Secular World*. Bronx, NY: Fordham University Press.

Dillon, Michael and Neal, Andrew W. (eds) (2008). *Foucault on Politics, Security and War*. New York: Palgrave Macmillan.

Dryzek, John (2006). *Deliberative Global Politics: Discourse and Democracy in a Divided World*. Cambridge: Polity Press.

During, Simon (ed.) (1999). *The Cultural Studies Reader*. 2nd edn. London and New York: Routledge.

Dworkin, Ronald (1985). *A Matter of Principle*. Cambridge, MA: Harvard University Press.

—(1986). *Law's Empire*. Cambridge, MA: Belknap Press.

Elster, Jon (2004). *Closing the Books: Transitional Justice in Historical Perspective*. Cambridge: Cambridge University Press.

Esposito, Roberto (2008). *Bios: Biopolitics and Philosophy*. Translated by Timothy Campbell. Minneapolis: University of Minnesota Press.

Ferejohn, John (2002). 'Judicializing Politics, Politicizing Law'. *Law and Contemporary Problems* 61: 41–68.

Ferrajoli, Luigi (2007). *Principia juris. Teoria del diritto e della democrazia*. 3 vols. Roma and Bari: Laterza.

160 References

Ferrara, Alessandro (1999). *Justice and Judgement: The Rise and the Prospect of the Judgement Model in Contemporary Political Philosophy*. London: Sage.

Ferrarese, Maria Rosaria (2006). *Diritto sconfinato. Inventiva giuridica e spazi nel mondo globale*. Roma and Bari: Laterza.

Fine, Robert (2007). *Cosmopolitanism*. Abingdon: Routledge.

Fioravanti, Maurizio (2009). *Costituzionalismo. Percorsi della storia e tendenze attuali*. Roma and Bari: Laterza.

Forst, Rainer (2002). *Contexts of Justice: Political Philosophy beyond Liberalism and Communitarianism*. Translated by John M. M. Farrell. Berkeley and Los Angeles: University of California Press.

Foucault, Michel (2007). *Security, Territory, Population: Lectures at the Collège de France 1977–1978*. Edited by Michel Senellart. Translated by Graham Burchell. New York: Palgrave Macmillan.

—(2008). *The Birth of Biopolitics: Lectures at the Collège de France 1978–1979*. Edited by Michel Senellart. Translated by Graham Burchell. New York: Palgrave Macmillan.

Fraser, Nancy and Honneth, Axel (2003). *Redistribution or Recognition? A Political-Philosophical Exchange*. London and New York: Verso.

Galli, Carlo (2010). *Political Spaces and Global War*. Edited by Adam Sitze. Translated by Elisabeth Fay. Minneapolis: University of Minnesota Press.

Gallino, Luciano (2011). *Finanzcapitalismo. La civiltà del denaro in crisi*. Torino: Einaudi.

Galtung, Johan (1996). *Peace by Peaceful Means: Peace and Conflict, Development and Civilization*. Oslo: International Peace Research Institute.

Garapon, Antoine (2002). *Des Crimes qu'on ne peut ni punir ni pardonner. Pour une justice internationale*. Paris: Odile Jacob.

—(2008). *Peut-on réparer l'Histoire? Colonisation, esclavage, Shoah*. Paris: Odile Jacob.

—(2010). *La Raison du moindre État. Le néolibéralisme et la justice*. Paris: Odile Jacob.

Gill, Stephen and Cutler, Claire A. (eds) (2014). *New Constitutionalism and World Order*. Cambridge: Cambridge University Press.

Golden, Ben and Fitzpatrick, Peter (2009). *Foucault's Law*. New York: Routledge.

Goodale, Mark and Merry, Sally Engle (2007). *The Practice of Human Rights: Tracking Law Between the Global and the Local*. Cambridge: Cambridge University Press.

Griffiths, John (1986). 'What is Legal Pluralism?' *Journal of Legal Pluralism and Unofficial Law* 24: 1–55.

Grossi, Paolo (2003). *Prima lezione di diritto*. Roma and Bari: Laterza.

—(2010). *A History of European Law*. Translated by Laurence Hooper. Malden, MA: Wiley-Blackwell.

Habermas, Jürgen (1996). *Between Facts and Norms: Contributions to a Discourse Theory of Law and Democracy*. Translated by William Rehg. Cambridge, MA: MIT Press.

—(1998). *The Inclusion of the Other: Studies in Political Theory*. Edited by Ciaran Cronin and Pablo De Greif. Cambridge, MA: MIT Press.

Habermas, Jürgen et al. (eds) (2010). *An Awareness of What is Missing: Faith and Reason in a Post-Secular Age*. Translated by Ciaran Cronin. Cambridge: Polity Press.

Hadden, Jeffrey K. (1987). 'Toward Desacralizing Secularization Theory'. *Social Forces* 65: 587–611.

Hardt, Michael and Negri, Antonio (2000). *Empire*. Cambridge, MA: Harvard University Press.

Harvey, David (2005). *A Brief History of Neoliberalism*. Oxford: Oxford University Press.

Heater, Derek (1996). *World Citizenship and Government: Cosmopolitan Ideas in the History of Western Political Thought*. New York: St Martin's Press.

Held, David (1995). *Democracy and the Global Order: From Modern State to Cosmopolitan Governance*. Cambridge: Polity Press.

—(2010). *Cosmopolitanism: Ideals and Realities*. Cambridge: Polity Press.

Hirschl, Ran (2004). *Toward Juristocracy: The Origins and Consequences of the New Constitutionalism*. Cambridge, MA: Harvard University Press.

—(2008). 'The Judicialization of Mega-Politics and the Rise of Political Courts'. *Annual Review of Political Science* 11: 93–118.

Honneth, Axel (1995). *The Struggle for Recognition: The Moral Grammar of Social Conflicts*. Translated by Joel Anderson. Cambridge, MA: MIT Press.

Honohan, Iseult (2002). *Civic Republicanism*. London and New York: Routledge.

Huntington, Samuel P. (1996). *The Clash of Civilizations and the Remaking of World Order*. New York: Simon & Schuster.

Kaldor, Mary (1999). *New and Old Wars: Organized Violence in a Global Era*. Oxford: Polity Press.

Krisch, Nico (2011). *Beyond Constitutionalism: The Pluralist Structure of Postnational Law*. Oxford: Oxford University Press.

Kritz, Neil J. (ed.) (1995). *Transitional Justice: How Emerging Democracies Reckon with Former Regimes*. 3 vols. Washington, DC: United States Institute of Peace.

Kuper, Adam (1999). *Culture: The Anthropologists' Account*. Cambridge, MA: Harvard University Press.

Kymlicka, Will (1995). *Multicultural Citizenship: A Liberal Theory of Minority Rights*. Oxford: Oxford University Press.

—(2007). *Multicultural Odysseys: Navigating the New International Politics of Diversity*. Oxford: Oxford University Press.

Lemke, Thomas (1997). *Eine Kritik der politischen Vernunft. Foucaults Analyse der modernen Gouvernementalität*. Berlin and Hamburg: Argument.

Lovett, Frank (2010). *A General Theory of Domination and Justice*. Oxford: Oxford University Press.

MacCormick, Neil (2007). *Institutions of Law: An Essay in Legal Theory*. Oxford: Oxford University Press.

MacIntyre, Alasdair (2007). *After Virtue: A Study in Moral Theory*. 3rd edn. Notre Dame, IN: University of Notre Dame Press.

Mann, Michael (2012). *The Sources of Social Power. Vol. 1: A History of Power from the Beginning to AD 1760*. Cambridge: Cambridge University Press.

Marchetti, Raffaele (2008). *Global Democracy: For and Against: Ethical Theory, Institutional Design, and Social Struggles*. Abingdon: Routledge.

Mattei, Ugo and Nader, Laura (2008). *Plunder: When the Rule of Law is Illegal*. Malden, MA: Blackwell.

Maynor, John W. (2003). *Republicanism in the Modern World*. Oxford: Blackwell.

Miller, David (2007). *National Responsibility and Global Justice*. Oxford: Oxford University Press.

Monbiot, George (2003). *The Age of Consent: A Manifesto for a New World Order*. London: Harper Perennial.

Moore, Sally F. (2000). *Law as Process: An Anthropological Approach*. Hamburg: LIT Verlag.

Morozov, Aleksandr (2008). 'Has the Postsecular Age Begun?' *Religion, State and Society* 36: 39–44.

Nagel, Thomas (2005). 'The Problem of Global Justice'. *Philosophy and Public Affairs* 33: 113–47.

Nino, Carlos S. (1996). *The Constitution of Deliberative Democracy*. New Haven, CT: Yale University Press.

Nussbaum, Martha C. (1997). *Cultivating Humanity: A Classical Defense of Reform in Liberal Education*. Cambridge, MA: Harvard University Press.

—(2001). *Upheavals of Thought: The Intelligence of Emotions*. Cambridge: Cambridge University Press.

Odysseos, Louiza and Petito, Fabio (eds) (2009). *The International Political Thought of Carl Schmitt: Terror, Liberal War and the Crisis of Global Order*. London: Routledge.

Pettit, Philip (1997). *Republicanism: A Theory of Freedom and Government*. Oxford: Oxford University Press.

Phillips, Anne (2007). *Multiculturalism without Culture*. Princeton, NJ: Princeton University Press.

Plant, Raymond (2010). *The Neo-liberal State*. Oxford: Oxford University Press.

Pogge, Thomas (2008). *World Poverty and Human Rights: Cosmopolitan Responsibilities and Reforms*. 2nd edn. Cambridge: Polity Press.

—(2010). *Politics as Usual: What Lies behind the Pro-Poor Rhetoric*. Cambridge: Polity Press.

Rajagopal, Balakrishnan (2003). *International Law from Below: Development, Social Movements and Third World Resistance*. Cambridge: Cambridge University Press.

Rawls, John (1971). *A Theory of Justice*. Cambridge, MA: Belknap Press of
    Harvard University Press.
—(1993). *Political Liberalism*. New York: Columbia University Press.
—(1999). *The Law of Peoples: With, The Idea of Public Reason Revisited*.
    Cambridge, MA: Harvard University Press.
Risse, Mathias (2012). *On Global Justice*. Princeton, NJ: Princeton
    University Press.
Rodrik, Dani (2011). *The Globalization Paradox: Democracy and the Future
    of the World Economy*. New York: W. W. Norton & Company.
Roht-Arriaza, Naomi and Mariezcurrena, Javier (eds) (2006). *Transitional
    Justice in the Twenty-First Century: Beyond Truth versus Justice*.
    Cambridge: Cambridge University Press.
Rorty, Richard (1989). *Contingency, Irony, and Solidarity*. Cambridge:
    Cambridge University Press.
Rosenau, James N. (2003). *Distant Proximities: Dynamics Beyond
    Globalization*. Princeton, NJ: Princeton University Press.
—(2006). *The Study of World Politics*. 2 vols. London and New York:
    Routledge.
Sandel, Michael (1998). *Liberalism and the Limits of Justice*. 2nd edn.
    Cambridge: Cambridge University Press.
Sassen, Saskia (2006). *Territory, Authority, Rights: From Medieval to Global
    Assemblages*. Princeton, NJ: Princeton University Press.
—(2007). *A Sociology of Globalization*. New York: W. W. Norton &
    Company.
Sen, Amartya (1992). *Inequality Reexamined*. Cambridge, MA: Harvard
    University Press.
—(2009). *The Idea of Justice*. Cambridge, MA: Harvard University Press.
Shachar, Ayelet (2001). *Multicultural Jurisdictions: Cultural Differences and
    Women's Rights*. Cambridge: Cambridge University Press.
Shaw, Martin (2005). *The New Western Way of War: Risk-Transfer War and
    its Crisis in Iraq*. Cambridge: Polity Press.
Singer, Peter W. (2003). *Corporate Warriors: The Rise of the Privatized
    Military Industry*. Ithaca: Cornell University Press.
Smith, Rupert (2005). *The Utility of Force: The Art of War in the Modern
    World*. London and New York: Allen Lane.

Sousa Santos, Boaventura de (1995). *Toward a New Common Sense: Law, Science and Politics in Paradigmatic Transition*. London and New York: Routledge.

Sousa Santos, Boaventura de and Rodríguez-Garavito, Cesar A. (eds) (2005). *Law and Globalization from Below: Towards a Cosmopolitan Legality*. Cambridge: Cambridge University Press.

Soysal, Yasemin N. (1994). *Limits of Citizenship: Migrants and Postnational Membership in Europe*. Chicago: The University of Chicago Press.

Stiglitz, Joseph E. (2002). *Globalization and Its Discontents*. New York: W. W. Norton & Company.

Stone Sweet, Alec (2000). *Governing with Judges: Constitutional Politics in Europe*. Oxford: Oxford University Press.

Strange, Susan (1996). *The Retreat of the State: The Diffusion of Power in the World Economy*. Cambridge: Cambridge University Press.

Streeck, Wolfgang (2014). *Buying Time: The Delayed Crisis of Democratic Capitalism*. Translated by Patrick Camiller. Brooklyn, NY: Verso.

Tamanaha, Brian Z. (2008). 'Understanding Legal Pluralism: Past to Present, Local to Global'. *Sydney Law Review* 30: 375–411.

Taylor, Charles (1989). *Sources of the Self: The Making of the Modern Identity*. Cambridge: Cambridge University Press.

—(2007). *A Secular Age*. Harvard, MA: The Belknap Press of Harvard University Press.

Teitel, Ruti G. (2002). *Transitional Justice*. Oxford: Oxford University Press.

Teubner, Günther (1991). 'The Two Faces of Janus: Rethinking Legal Pluralism'. *Cardozo Law Review* 13: 1443–62.

—(2004). 'Societal Constitutionalism: Alternatives to State-centred Constitutional Theory?' In *Transnational Governance and Constitutionalism*. Edited by Christian Joerges, Inger-Johann Sand and Günther Teubner, 3–28. Oxford and Portland, OR: Hart.

Thornton, Rod (2007). *Asymmetric Warfare: Threat and Response in the 21ˢᵗ Century*. Cambridge: Polity Press.

Twining, William (2009a). *General Jurisprudence: Understanding Law from a Global Perspective*. Cambridge: Cambridge University Press.

—(ed.) (2009b). *Human Rights: Southern Voices*. Cambridge: Cambridge University Press.

Van Creveld, Martin L. (1991). *The Transformation of War*. New York: Free Press.

Waldron, Jeremy (1995). 'Minority Cultures and the Cosmopolitan Alternative'. In *The Rights of Minority Cultures*. Edited by Will Kymlicka, 93–119. Oxford: Oxford University Press.

Waltz, Kenneth N. (1979). *Theory of International Politics*. Boston: McGraw-Hill.

Walzer, Michael (1983). *Spheres of Justice: A Defense of Pluralism and Equality*. New York: Basic Books.

—(1997). *On Toleration*. New Haven, CT: Yale University Press.

Woodman, Gordon R. (2009). 'Diritto consuetudinario e diritti consuetudinari: una considerazione comparativa sulla loro natura e sulle relazioni tra tipi di diritto'. *Politica & Società* 2: 91–107.

Zagrebelsky, Gustavo (1992). *Il diritto mite. Legge, diritti, giustizia*. Torino: Einaudi.

Zolo, Danilo (2002). *Invoking Humanity: War, Law and Global Order*. London: Continuum.

—(2009). *Victors' Justice: From Nuremberg to Baghdad*. London: Verso.

Index

validity 36–7, 139–40
  formal 32, 37
  legal 33, 36, 40–1, 127, 141, 147
  normative 29
  substantial 32, 37
Van Creveld, Martin 68
vernacularization 100–1
violence 11, 24, 76, 82, 95, 97, 101, 103, 128
  privatization of 66–70
  structural 64–5, 77

Waldron, Jeremy 92
Waltz, Kenneth 102–3
Walzer, Michael 9–10, 12, 64
  Spheres of Justice 10–11
war 55, 75
  asymmetric 66, 68
  civil 53, 68
  Cold 52, 65–6, 68, 110
  confessional 111

crimes of 49, 51–4
Gulf 69
modern 65
moralized 98
neo-colonial 101
new 65–70, 93
religious 101
resort to 61
on terrorism 16
World x, 7, 29, 52, 96, 98, 129
welfare xi, 7, 152
Woodman, Gordon R. 138, 141–4
workers 12, 61, 63, 79
World Assembly 96
World Bank 49
world risk society 81–2
WTO 49, 88

Zagrebelsky, Gustavo 32
Zeno of Citium 90, 102
Žižek, Slavoj 102
Zolo, Danilo 54, 98